Borderland Jaguars

Borderland

Tigres

David E. Brown

Salt Lake City

Jaguars
de la Frontera

Carlos A. López González

THE UNIVERSITY OF UTAH PRESS

Library of Congress Cataloging-in-Publication Data

Brown, David E. (David Earl), 1938–
    Bordlerland Jaguars = Tigres de la frontera /
David E. Brown and Carlos A. López González.
        p.   cm.
Includes bibliographical references.
    ISBN 0-87480-696-8 (pbk. : alk. paper)
    1. Jaguar—Mexican-American Border Region.
I. Title: Tigres de la frontera. II. López González, Carlos A., 1966–
III. Title.
    QL737.C23 B78 2001
    599.75'5—dc21
                                    2001003861

Contents

Preface   vii
Introduction   1

1. Natural History   15
    Physical Description   15
    Subspecies   28
    Fossil Record   30
    Distribution   32
    Habitats   43
    Prey   50
    Breeding and Reproduction   55
    Population Characteristics of Southwestern Jaguars   57
    Home Ranges and Coexistence with Other Carnivores   60
    Status of Other Borderland Cats   63

2. Jaguars and People   67
    The Jaguar in Prehistoric Cultures   68
    The Jaguar in Contemporary Southwestern Native Cultures   80
    Anglo Americans and Borderland Jaguars   85
    Jaguars in Northern Sonora   100
    Hunting Jaguars   110
    Jaguars in Borderland Folklore   128
    The Jaguar as a Symbol   132

3. Status and Conservation   137
    Management History   137
    Jaguars in Texas and Tamaulipas   141
    Proposed Jaguar Conservation Plan   142

Appendix 1: County bounty ledger and affidavit form
    used in Texas for paying out bounties in 1913   145

Appendix 2: Annual report of game killed in 1917 on the
    National Forests of the Southwestern District, Arizona   146
Appendix 3: Big game killed on Coronado National Forest,
    Arizona, in 1920   147

Bibliography   149
Acknowledgments   161
Index   165

Preface

> We saw neither hide nor hair of him, but his personality
> pervaded the wilderness; no living beast forgot his potential
> presence, for the price of unwariness was death. No deer
> rounded a bush, or stopped to nibble pods under a mesquite
> tree, without a premonitory sniff for *el tigre.* No campfire
> died without talk of him.
>
> Aldo Leopold (1949) "The Green Lagoons"
> in *A Sand County Almanac*

The faded blanket that served as a door was tied back as far as possible, and the concrete floor and high ceiling were designed for July days such as this. Yet the house was stifling almost beyond endurance. Not the slightest breeze entered the room, which was a literal oven. Sweat exuded from every pore, but brought no noticeable relief. The conversation droned on as if we were in a dream that had no beginning or end.

We were in Mexico's state of Sonora with the self-assigned task of finding out if any jaguars were present. Our host, a local man who appeared to be in his late thirties, was reputed to have recently killed one. Now, heedless of the heat, he was enthusiastically describing his encounter with the jaguar, whose skull was said to be in the adjoining bedroom. Whenever his account lagged for even the briefest moment, his wife or daughter would jump in to supply the missing details of a story they had heard a dozen times. Killing a *tigre* is, after all, the highlight of a man's life—a trait we found shared by a small cadre of countrymen on both sides of the border. Enthused by his own recollections and encouraged by the rapt attention of his audience, the man gradually let his wariness subside. Suddenly, as if forgetting something, he wheeled around and disappeared into the bedroom.

In less than a minute he was back with the jaguar skull, a mountain lion skull, and what he said was the pelt of a baby jaguar. All three of these items were dutifully fondled before being passed on to us so that we too might feel the texture and power contained within. Taking the two skulls and laying them upside down, we demonstrated how one can quickly tell a *tigre* skull from that of a *león* (the name for a mountain lion in rural Mexico) by looking for the fingerlike projection in the jaguar skull's palate. Our host understood the difference immediately and beamed his appreciation of the shared knowledge. Perhaps this *chilango* (a Mexican born in Mexico City) and his *gringo* companion knew something about jaguars after all.

Carlos López and I have looked at a lot of jaguar skulls, both before and since that sweltering afternoon in Sahuaripa, Sonora. I had first became interested in these big cats in November 1965, when I answered a call to the Tucson office of the Arizona Game and Fish Department from a man requesting a bounty on a jaguar he had taken while deer hunting near the Mexican border. Although no bounty was forthcoming, the taking of the animal had been perfectly legal, prompting a then-young wildlife manager to visit the local taxidermist to see what a wild jaguar looked like. And although this jaguar was not a particularly large specimen, its pale background and complex pattern of spots and dashes made the animal more than merely handsome. The jaguar, and all it represented, was nothing if not enchanting. For who can view one of these cats and not become transfixed by its presence?

Having been secondarily involved in this tropical incursion, I then began investigating and collecting other jaguar records, not only from Arizona, but also from the animals' supposed source in the adjacent Mexican state of Sonora. One report led to another, and an odyssey of trailing jaguars and jaguar hunters began, a journey that entailed not only traveling from one locale to another, but also going back through time. Collecting borderland jaguar lore became a hobby and then an avocation, and in 1983 I published a summary of jaguar incursions into Arizona and New Mexico in the *Southwestern Naturalist*. Since then, Carlos López and I have sought out and interviewed almost every living person who has had a bona fide encounter with a jaguar in Arizona. And for every jaguar, there was a jaguar story, several of which have been published in magazines such as *Pacific Discovery, Rocky Mountain Sportsman,* and *Defenders*. These articles, although informative, lacked many interesting details, and with several more incursions having since taken place, it is now time to present a fuller story and summarize the animal's shaky tenure in the American Southwest.

Carlos López's interests, while more recent, have been of a more scientific nature. Working as a field biologist in the Mexican states of Veracruz and Quintana Roo in 1989, he soon became aware of the plethora of conservation problems attendant with jaguars and jaguar habitat in Mexico. In 1992 his interest in big cats intensified while he was working as a field assistant on a study of white-tailed deer in the tropical deciduous forests of the Chamela-Cuixmala Biosphere Reserve in the state of Jalisco. After doing research in an area with six different felids, Carlos López became so involved with cats that he eventually pursued a doctoral degree using data he obtained studying mountain lions in Idaho from 1991 to 1996. Now armed with experience in cat biology, he returned to Chamela-Cuixmala in 1994 to become the principal investigator to study the interactions of jaguars, pumas, ocelots, bobcats, and jaguarundis. In 1998 I appointed Carlos López chief investigator of a jaguar study in the state of Sonora. We have been investigating jaguars and jaguar habitats ever since.

Although we can summarize the status of jaguars in Arizona and New Mexico and present our findings about those jaguars still persisting in Sonora, the jaguar's role in the Southwest continues to unfold. Our current knowledge about these cats is fragmentary, and much of the animal's basic life-history information is lacking or incomplete. Due to the enormous difficulties attendant with studying jaguars in Sonora, some biological information may never be known. Nor is the continued presence of this cat in Sonora by any means certain—the jaguar's penchant for dining on livestock invites constant persecution. And should the jaguar disappear from Sonora, as the animal has from so many other areas, there will be no more incursions into Arizona, New Mexico, or Chihuahua to report. Therefore, we hope that this background summary of the jaguar's history, accompanied by our imperfect understanding of these *tigres norteños,* will measurably contribute to their conservation. With no Sonoran *tigres,* the story of borderland jaguars never will be unravelled, and the accompanying lore that continues to fascinate us, and hopefully you, will cease. So, while there is still time and while jaguars are still to be found in the borderlands of the Southwest, come join the hunt.

David E. Brown

Introduction

Around the campfires of Mexico there is no animal talked
about, nor more romanticized and glamorized, than *el tigre*.
The chesty roar of a jaguar in the night causes men to edge toward the blaze and draw serapes tighter. It silences the yapping
dogs and starts the tethered horses milling. In announcing its
mere presence in the blackness of night, the jaguar puts the
animate world on edge. For this very reason it is the most
interesting and exciting of all the wild animals of Mexico.
                     A. Starker Leopold (1959) *Wildlife of Mexico*

On March 7, 1996, a remarkable event occurred. Accompanied by
his daughter, Kelly, and an assistant named Aaron Prudler, rancher Warner
Glenn was hunting mountain lions for a client named Al Kriedeman.
Their hunting ground was east of Glenn's Malpai Ranch just north of the
Mexican border in the Peloncillo ("Little Baldy") Mountains, which strad-
dle the Arizona–New Mexico border. This fourth day of the hunt was clear
but windy. They had hardly set out when Kelly radioed her father to hurry
over because the strike dog, Maple, had just jumped a big lion.

Galloping up to the main ridge of the Peloncillos on his mule, Snowy
River, Glenn and five more hounds set out to intercept the cat. The country was rugged, full of brush, and rimmed with boulders, but the cat
seemed tireless and unwilling to either tree or come to bay. The incessant
wind not only made it hard for the dogs to follow the cat's scent, but it
blew away the sound of their yapping chorus, causing Glenn to fear either
the dogs' losing the cat or his losing the dogs. Following the pack and what
he still assumed was a big tom lion, Glenn and Snowy River soon left their
companions far behind. Finally, after a chase of several miles, the cat
sought refuge on a high bluff out of reach of his tormentors, which were
bawling and jumping below him.

Spotting the cat from afar, Glenn tied Snowy River to a stout limb and headed down toward the commotion. As he peered through the Mexican piñons and shrubbery, he could hardly believe his eyes. There, crouched atop the bluff, was not a tom lion but a full-grown jaguar. Glenn clambered back up to his mule to retrieve the camera he kept in a pouch tied to his saddle horn.

What followed was a merry chase through the rocks, the jaguar alternately fighting the dogs and then jumping onto another outcrop or into a crevice. After shooting a few photographs (see Plates 1 and 2), Glenn could see that his biggest problem was going to be how to separate the dogs from the jaguar before one of them got seriously hurt. By now the pandemonium was at a crescendo, the jaguar's roars mixing with the dogs' howling. Adding to the sense of bedlam, as it had throughout the pursuit, was the constant odor of skunk. Apparently, the jaguar had either been involved in an unwelcome altercation or had been hard up for his most recent meal.

Snapping pictures with his right hand and pulling off dogs with his left, Glenn waded into the fray. Cornered and frantic to escape, the jaguar would have run over him but for the aggressiveness of the hounds. The melee raged on, neither side getting the upper hand. Then suddenly the battle was over, the jaguar heading at a trot back into Mexico.

Miraculously, the jaguar's retreat was accomplished without any fatalities. Only three of the hounds had been injured, none seriously. The worst wound was a bite through Maple's left hind leg, which had broken a bone. Two other dogs had been clawed, but neither was bleeding badly. It was not yet noon, but Warner Glenn's hunt was over. The experience, he says, "fulfilled a lifelong dream for me." So satisfied was he with his adventure that he immediately set about writing a memoir to accompany the photographs he prayed would come out. Glenn called his book *Eyes of Fire,* a title that was to prove appropriate.

The repercussions resulting from Warner Glenn's adventure are difficult to overstate. His book and photographs were soon on display in every bookstore from Phoenix to El Paso, not to mention ranch-house living rooms and the lobby of the Gadsen Hotel in Douglas, Arizona. These compelling photographs and the story that accompanied them generated a widespread public interest in borderland jaguars. Later that summer, when Jack Childs and another party of houndsmen photographed a jaguar they had treed in Arizona's Baboquivari Mountains (Figure 1), the event was almost an anticlimax.

Two questions were now on everyone's mind: Where had these jaguars come from? And what could be done to perpetuate their presence? Federal

Figure 1. Treed jaguar photographed on August 31, 1996, by Jack Childs and party in the Baboquivari Mountains, Arizona.

officials were pressured to complete the process of listing the jaguar as an endangered species in the United States, and state bureaucrats, fearful of potential legal restrictions, hastily formed a Jaguar Conservation Team of experts and interested parties to ruminate over how to manage these large cats without federal involvement. What was especially remarkable, however, was not so much the occurrence of jaguars in the American Southwest, which had happened dozens of times before, but the outcome of the two hunts: For the first time the animal's presence had been documented with photographs instead of the cat being killed. Now everybody had reason to hope that Glenn's and Child's experiences would not be the last.

What is it about these borderland cats that has so fired up people? Scarcity combined with beauty certainly explains some of the jaguar's appeal. So does the animal's legendary strength and power, as befits its role as the region's top predator. The jaguar's neotropical origins also add to its mystique. There is always something inherently romantic about an exotic visitor from the south. But there is something more: The knowledge that such a large cat is out there somewhere, or is at least thought to be, invokes the depths of our imagination. It doesn't matter one whit that the chance of anyone actually seeing a jaguar is almost nil. The thought of such a cat's presence is enough in itself.

That the jaguar comes with a reputation cannot be denied. Yet much of the animal's eminence is more symbolic than real. The animal itself is almost never heard or seen. And so desirous are people of seeing one that those who do can rarely be regarded as reliable. One can truthfully say that, until very recently, a jaguar had to be killed to be believed—thus, the necessity for the procession of dead jaguars portrayed in this book. But these depictions are also essential for the telling of the story if for no other reason than, with rare exceptions, the only people who have had any contact with borderland jaguars during the last century have been hunters and ranchmen. To these people, who value the jaguar as much or more than any of us, to appreciate a jaguar has always been to kill it. Naturalists and wildlife photographers usually ply their trade in national parks and refuges, not while roaming about rangelands and cow carcasses, and no refuge for jaguars has ever existed in the Southwest.

Known throughout Mexico and other Spanish-speaking countries as *el tigre* and as *onça (onza)* in Portuguese-speaking Brazil, even the animal's names come with a romantic ring. Its English name, jaguar, is said to come from the word *yaguara* in the Tupi-Guarani language of Amazonia, which has been variously reported to mean "eater of us," "body of a dog," and most recently, "the wild beast that overcomes its prey at a bound" (Hoogesteijn and Mondolfi 1993). Although jaguars have long been subjects of fascination along the U.S.-Mexico border, this exotic term is of relatively recent derivation. In Mexico the animal has always been known as *el tigre,* and prior to World War I, those frontier Americans not simply using the English "tiger" rather than the Spanish *tigre* commonly referred to the jaguar as an "American leopard" or "Mexican leopard." These latter names reflect well the animal's appearance, its habits, and even its evolutionary history. In fact, taxonomists place the two species in the same genus: the leopard is *Panthera pardus,* the jaguar *Panthera onca.* The jaguar's species name, *onca,* was originally a Greek word for the European lynx.

Because the jaguar's range in the Southwest has always been shared with the mountain lion *(Puma concolor),* it may be best to clarify our terminology for this other multinamed cat. When we are referring to this cat in the American Southwest (or, the Mexican Northwest), we will use the popularly accepted name of "mountain lion" or *león.* When we speak of

Figure 2. Mounted jaguar in the American Museum of Natural History in New York City. The cat was taken in 1940 from the Sierra Bacatete, Sonora.

this cat farther south in Central and South America, we use the equivalent term of "puma."

In this book, we consider "borderland jaguars" to be those jaguars found in the southwestern American states of Arizona and New Mexico and the northwestern Mexican states of Sonora and Chihuahua. Although our primary topic is borderland jaguars, we will also present information on jaguars in Texas and several neighboring Mexican states.

During the twentieth century, more than sixty jaguars reportedly were taken in Arizona and New Mexico. At least four of these animals were females. Biologists such as E. A. Goldman (1932, 1939) and Donald F. Hoffmeister (1986) believed that the jaguar was a resident of Arizona as well as Texas. It has long been known in both official and unofficial circles that jaguars were present immediately to the south in Sonora, Mexico (Figure 2). But the recent status of these animals was poorly known until we investigated the past and present occurrences of jaguars on both sides of the border.

Working both in the field and in the library, we have examined as many Southwestern jaguars as possible and inspected all of the hides and skulls available to us. We have also visited numerous museums and archeological sites having jaguar artifacts and interviewed many of the people who have killed jaguars, both in Sonora and Arizona. The result is not only the most complete documentation of the jaguar's historic occurrence in the Southwest, but the largest series of borderland jaguar photographs ever assembled. More importantly, our research on this great cat has provided us with the beginnings of some much-needed information on the jaguar's life history and habits in this area, enough so that we can make some statements as to the cat's present and future status in this region.

We are not the first to chronicle occurrences of this always-noteworthy cat in the American Southwest. Ernest Thompson Seton (1919, 1920, 1929), Vernon Bailey (1905, 1931, 1935), Kenneth I. Lange (1960), and Bob Housholder (1958, 1975) all tabulated jaguar records—a shared affliction for which we are very grateful. Agency personnel have also provided individual jaguar accounts and periodically prepared lists of jaguar records and literature references. These efforts notwithstanding, the most comprehensive summaries of information on borderland jaguars is contained within Tables 1 and 2. We also document for the first time jaguars killed in the Mexican state of Chihuahua (Table 3). All of the records presented here are of dead, captured, or photographed jaguars. Jaguars taken on guided hunts that may have involved released animals are not included, nor are unverifiable sightings.

One question remains, however. Was the jaguar a resident animal during historical times in the American Southwest, or has it always been a transient from Mexico? One can argue the evidence on this intriguing topic both ways, and biologists will continue to disagree as to the animal's historical status. We are not yet certain as to the answer to this question, but future work on DNA samples taken from borderland jaguars may someday shed light on this enigma. In the meantime, read this book and judge for yourself.

Table 1. Jaguars reportedly killed or photographed
in Arizona and New Mexico, 1900–2000.[1]

Date	Collector and Documentation	Sex	Location and Circumstances	Biotic Community[2]
8/31/1996	Jack Childs. Pers. comm., Childs 1998, AGFD files. Photographs.	M?	Baboquivari Mts., AZ. Treed and photographed while lion hunting with dogs.	Madrean evergreen woodland
3/07/1996	Warner Glenn. Pers. comm., Glenn 1996. Photographs.	M?	Peloncillo Mts., AZ. Bayed and photographed while lion hunting with dogs.	Madrean evergreen woodland

Date	Collector and Documentation	Sex	Location and Circumstances	Biotic Community[2]
12/1986	J. Klump et al. AGFD files, USFWS files. Photographs.	M	Dos Cabezas Mts., AZ. Bayed and killed while lion hunting with dogs. Wt. = 138 lb.	Madrean evergreen woodland?
11/16/1971	R. Farley and T. Cartier. Pers. comm. Santa Cruz Co. court records. Photographs.	M	S of Hwy 82, Santa Cruz River, AZ. Killed by boys duck hunting with shotguns. Stomach "full of frogs." Head, eviscerated carcass, and hide = 130 lb, TL = 72 in.	semidesert grassland/ Madrean evergreen woodland
11/16/1965	Laurence McGee. Pers. comm. Photographs, skull at University of Arizona.	M	Patagonia Mts., AZ. Shot while deer hunting. Dressed wt. = 88 lb, TL = 70 in.	Madrean evergreen woodland
1/16/1964	PARC agent Russell Culbreath. Pers. comm., USFWS files. Photographs.	M	SW of ID Ranch on breaks above Black River, WMAIR, AZ. Trapped by predator control agent.	semidesert grassland/ Great Basin conifer woodland
9/28/1963	Terry Penrod. Pers. comm. Photographs.	F	At 9000 ft, S of Big Lake, White Mts., AZ. Shot while predator calling. Had fed on elk carrion. Whole wt. = 105 lb, dressed wt. = 78 lbs.	Rocky Mt. montane/ subalpine conifer forest
7/26/1961	H. Barnett, Ed Hilton, T. Ferguson, S. Goodwin. Pers. comm., Barnett 1961. Photographs.	M	Total Wreck Mine, Empire Mts., AZ. Bayed with dogs and shot as stock killer. TL = 75 in.	semidesert grassland/ riparian
10 or 11/1957	Mr. Ferguson fide Sewell Goodwin and P. Cosper.	M	Red Mt. near Clifton, AZ. Shot while deer hunting.	chaparral/Madrean evergreen woodland
winter 1956–1957	Jimmy Gilbert. Skull at University of Arizona.	M?	White River, WMAIR, AZ.	riparian/Great Basin conifer woodland
11/13/1949	Walter Noon. Arizona Daily Star (11/15/1949), Heald 1955, Hock 1955, Housholder 1958. Photographs.	F	Cerro Colorado, AZ. Shot while deer hunting. Wt. = 110 lb, TL = 74 in.	semidesert grassland
spring 1948	Ray Harshman. Housholder 1958, 1974.	M	S of Patagonia, AZ. Bayed with hounds and shot by predator trapper.	Madrean evergreen woodland
1947	Jim Converse? Housholder 1974 fide AGFD Ranger G. Peterson.	?	Tumacacori Mts., AZ. Killed a big heifer; other circumstances unknown.	Madrean evergreen woodland
ca. 1940	Lavern West fide Steve Smith, Payson, AZ. Personal interview 8/9/2000.	?	Trout Creek, WMAIR, AZ. Taken with dogs?	riparian within Rocky Mt. montane conifer forest
11/23/1939	Red Harris. S. Goodwin, pers. comm., Housholder 1974. Photograph.	M	Ramanote Canyon, Atascosa Mts., AZ. Bayed with dogs and shot as stock killer.	Madrean evergreen woodland
1939	Unknown trapper. Lange 1960 fide H. C. Lockett.	?	Bloody Basin, AZ. Trapped.	semidesert grassland/ chaparral
1934	Unknown hunter. Lange 1960 fide Frank Hibben.	?	Atascosa Mts., AZ. Circumstances unknown.	Madrean evergreen woodland
1933	Unknown rancher. Arizona Republic, Housholder 1958.	?	Sierra Estrella foothills, AZ. Circumstances unknown.	Sonoran desertscrub
1932 or 1933	Frank Colcord (PARC). USFWS files, Housholder 1974, John Windes, pers. comm.	M	Patagonia Mts., AZ. Taken with dogs as stock killer.	Madrean evergreen woodland
1932	Unknown. Lange 1960 fide H. C. Lockett, Housholder 1958.	F	Grand Canyon Village, AZ. Taken by predator control agent in pine forest.	Rocky Mt. conifer forest
1928 or 1929	Unknown. Lange 1960 fide H. C. Lockett; fresh hide seen.	?	Sand Tank Mts., AZ. Circumstances unknown.	Sonoran desertscrub

Table 1. Jaguars reportedly killed or photographed in Arizona and New Mexico, 1900–2000 (continued).

Date	Collector and Documentation	Sex	Location and Circumstances	Biotic Community[2]
1926–1930	Unknown. Lange 1960 *fide* H. C. Lockett.	?	Chiricahua Mts., AZ. Circumstances unknown.	Madrean evergreen woodland?
12/1926	Clyde Miller. Lange 1960 *fide* M. E. Musgrave (PARC). Photograph.	M	NE slopes of Santa Maria Mts., AZ (near Prescott). Taken by rancher.	Rocky Mt. conifer forest/Great Basin conifer woodland
11/30/1926	Fred Ott (PARC). USFWS files, Housholder 1958, Lange 1960. Skull no. 247337 in USNM.	M	S of Patagonia, AZ. Taken with poison as a stock killer. "Adult."	Madrean evergreen woodland
1926	Fred Ott (PARC). USFWS files, Housholder 1958, Lange 1960. Skull in USNM.	?	S of Patagonia, AZ. Taken with poison as stock killer.	Madrean evergreen woodland
4/12/1924	Jack Funk (PARC). This animal is the type specimen for the *arizonensis* spp. USNM, Nelson and Goldman 1933.	M	Near Cibeque, WMAIR, AZ. Taken with hounds as stock killer.	Great Basin conifer woodland
1922	Frederick O. Knipe et al. *fide* Henrietta Barassi (granddaughter). Photograph.	?	Rincon Valley, AZ. Taken by rancher.	semidesert grassland?
1920	Unknown. Lange 1960 *fide* V. Bailey, USFS files.	?	"Killed" W of Santa Rita Mts., AZ.	semidesert grassland/ Madrean evergreen woodland
1/1920	Stanley R. Graham and party. Seton 1929, Lange 1960, *Holbrook Observer*, USFS files.	?	"Killed" in Rincon Mts., AZ.	Madrean evergreen woodland?
4/22/1919	R. Lee Parker (PARC). USFS files, Housholder 1958. Skin and skull in USNM.	F	Greaterville (Santa Rita Mts.), AZ. Trapped as stock killer. "Adult."	Madrean evergreen woodland
1918	Unknown trapper. Lange 1960 *fide* S. P. Young.	?	Base of Mt. Baldy (7000 ft), Santa Rita Mts., AZ.	Madrean evergreen woodland/Rocky Mt. montane conifer forest
1909–1918	Unknown. Lange 1960 *fide* E. W. Nelson.	?	Grand Canyon, AZ. Circumstances unknown.	Great Basin conifer woodland?
5/11/1917	E. J. O'Doherty (PARC). Nelson and Goldman 1933, Housholder 1958, Lange 1960, USFS files. Skull in USNM.	M	Helvetia (Santa Rita Mts.), AZ. Trapped as stock killer.	Madrean evergreen woodland
1916	Unknown "Mexican." Skin obtained by W. F. Cody for his ranch at Campo Bonita. USFS files.	M	Upper Canada del Oro, Catalina Mts., AZ. Trapped?	riparian/Madrean evergreen woodland/Rocky Mt. montane conifer forest
1913	Unknown deer hunter. *fide* B. V. Lily *in* Carmony 1998.	M	Red Mt. N of Clifton, AZ.	chaparral/ Madrean evergreen woodland
1913	J. H. Durham. Lange 1960 *fide* E. A. Goldman and E. T. Seton (1929), who saw the skin.	?	Tortolita Mts. (Durham Hills?), AZ. Killed by rancher. Circumstances unknown.	Sonoran desertscrub/ semidesert grassland
1912	Unknown. Lange 1960 *fide* C. T. Vorhies.	?	Rincon Mts., AZ. Circumstances unknown.	Madrean evergreen woodland?
ca. 1912	Unknown. Lange 1960 *fide* C. T. Vorhies, Seton 1929.	?	Canyon del Oro, Catalina Mts. Shot while feeding on prospector's burro.	Madrean evergreen woodland?
1912	O. Bozarth and E. Contreras. Housholder 1958, Lange 1960.	?	65 mi NW of Prescott on Bozarth Mesa, AZ. "Adult" animal roped and killed with rocks.	semidesert grassland/ chaparral
2/1912	Lon King. Lange 1960 *fide* E. W. Nelson.	? ??	W of Sunset Pass SW of Winslow, AZ. Two jaguars poisoned as stock killers.	Great Basin conifer woodland/Rocky Mt. montane conifer forest

Date	Collector and Documentation	Sex	Location and Circumstances	Biotic Community[2]
1/12/1912	Frank Hands. Calahane 1939, O'Conner 1939, Housholder 1958, Lange 1960. Hands diary and photographs by Riggs family; hide with skull in possession of Ted Troller, Portal, AZ.	M?	Bonita Canyon, Chiricahua Mts., AZ. Trapped before being trailed and bayed with hounds during snowstorm. Described as "him" by Percy Hands in Seton (1929). TL = 93 in.	Madrean evergreen woodland
1900–1912	Unknown. Seton 1929.	?	Baboquivari Mts., AZ.	Madrean evergreen woodland
1910	Unknown cowboy. Housholder 1958 fide AGFD Ranger R. Morrow. Lange 1960, Seton 1929?	F	Fly Peak, Chiricahua Mts., AZ.	Rocky Mt. montane conifer forest
10/1910	George Winslow. Lange 1960 fide E. W. Nelson.	F + cub	Head of Chevlon Canyon, AZ. Female and one young animal.	Rocky Mt. montane conifer forest
1909	Unknown hunter. B. V. Lilly in Carmony 1998.	?	Dog Springs, SE of Animas Mts., NM.	semidesert grassland
winter 1907–1908	Hopi Indians. Hoffmeister 1971 fide E. A. Goldman and E. Kolb. This is almost certainly the animal photographed in Billingsley 1971.	?	4 mi S of Grand Canyon, AZ. "Old" animal tracked and killed on snow in pine forest.	Rocky Mt. montane conifer forest/Great Basin conifer woodland
ca. 1907	Unknown. Seton 1929 fide Dr. Harry Garcelon, Lange 1960 fide V. Bailey.	?	Mogollon Mts., near Fort Apache, WMAIR, AZ.	Rocky Mt. montane conifer forest
1904–1907	Unknown. Lange 1960 fide V. Bailey and R. L. Parker.	2 ??	Patagonia Mts., AZ. Two jaguars killed; circumstances unknown.	Madrean evergreen woodland
5/31/1906	Unknown "Mexicans." Arizona Daily Star 6/1/1906.	F + 2 cubs	Chiricahua Mts., AZ. Female trapped and cubs offered for sale.	Madrean evergreen woodland?
1904–1905	Hunter named Morris. Bailey 1931.	?	W slopes of Sierra de los Caballos, NM.	semidesert grassland/ Great Basin conifer woodland
ca. 1904	Mr. West. Housholder 1977, pers. comm.	?	Verde River near Camp Verde, AZ.	riparian/semidesert grassland/chaparral
10/1903	Unknown. American Field (60:340), Lange 1960.	?	Atascosa Mts., AZ	Madrean evergreen woodland
1903	Unknown rancher. Bailey 1931.	?	Clanton Canyon, 6 mi W of Gray Ranch, Peloncillo Mts., NM. Shot while feeding on a bull.	Madrean evergreen woodland
1902	Unknown. Bailey 1931. Hide observed by Bailey.	?	Otero Co., NM. Given to Governor Otero.	?
1902	Monroe Copelen. USFS files.	?	Canada del Oro, Catalina Mts., AZ. Circumstances unknown.	riparian/Madrean evergreen woodland
8/1902	Mrs. Manning. Bailey 1931. Photographed by Ned Hollister.	?	Manning Ranch, Datil Mts., NM. Poisoned as a stock killer. "Adult."	Rocky Mt. montane conifer forest
3/16/1902	"Mexican bounty hunters." Schufeldt 1921. Arizona Historical Society photograph.	M	Rincon Mts., AZ. Bayed with dogs and shot.	Madrean evergreen woodland/Rocky Mt. montane conifer forest
6/1901	J. C. Riggs and a man named Ross. Lange 1960 fide E. J. Hands.	?	Dos Cabezas Mts., AZ.	Madrean evergreen woodland
5/1900	Nat Straw. Barber 1902, Bailey 1931.	?	Taylor Creek, Mogollon Mts., NM. Trapped by predator hunter.	riparian/Rocky Mt. montane conifer forest

1. Does not include guided hunts.

2. Biotic communities from Brown (1994).

Abbreviation key: AGFD, Arizona Game and Fish Department; PARC, Predator and Rodent Control Division of the U.S. Fish and Wildlife Service (after 1960) or U.S. Biological Survey (before 1960); TL, length from nose to tip of tail; USFS, U.S. Forest Service; USFWS, U.S. Fish and Wildlife Service; USNM, U.S. National Museum; WMAIR, White Mountain Apache Indian Reservation

Table 2. Jaguars reportedly killed or captured in Sonora, 1900–2000.

Date	Collector or Reporter	Sex	Location/Municipo	Biotic Community[1]
10/2000	Shot by vaquero while traveling. Skins in his possession.	F + 2 cubs	Ejido Badesi, Sahuaripa	Sinaloan thornscrub
10/2000	Killed. Skin in Hermosillo.	M	CFE property; Sahuaripa/Nacori Chico	Sinaloan thornscrub
09/2000	Killed. Skin in Hermosillo.	M	Rancho at km 55 on Mexican Hwy 15	Sinaloan thornscrub/ semidesert grassland
06/2000	Skull in La Estrella; skin in Soyopa.	M	Sierra El Novillo, San Pedro del la Cueva	Sinaloan thornscrub
5/2000	Shot by ranchman while cat was feeding on a cow.	M	Sierra Zetasora, Sahuaripa	Madrean evergreen woodland
01/2000	Stoned to death by vaqueros. Skin sold in Hermosillo.	M	Ejido Basopa, Sahuaripa	Sinaloan thornscrub
11/1999	Female chased away from dead cow.	F + 2 cubs	Rancho Los Pavos, Sahuaripa	Sinaloan thornscrub
07/1999	Poisoned as stock killer.	F	Rancho La Primavera, Sahuaripa	?
07/1999	Unknown circumstances. Photograph.	M	Nacori Chico	Sinaloan thornscrub
07/1999	Killed as stock killer. Skull < 7 months of age.	M	Rancho Los Pavos, Sierra Los Chinos, Sahuaripa	Sinaloan thornscrub
07/1999	Killed as stock killer; accompanied by cub that escaped.	F	Rancho Los Pavos, Sierra Los Chinos, Sahuaripa	Sinaloan thornscrub
05/1999	Killed as stock killer. Photograph.	F	Carrizal Quemado, Granados	Sinaloan thornscrub
05/1999	Found dead.	?	Rancho Badesi, Sierra Los Chinos, Sahuaripa	Sinaloan thornscrub
1999	Killed by ranchers as stock killer. Smuggled into United States.	F + 2 cubs	Sahuaripa/Nacori Chico	Sinaloan thornscrub
05/1998	Killed by lion hunter as a stock killer. Pers. comm.	F + cub	Rancho Los Pescador, Nacori Chico/Bacadehuachi	Sinaloan thornscrub
05/1998	Trapped by rancher as a stock killer. Pers. comm.	M	Rancho El Naranjo, Quiriego	Sinaloan thornscrub
1998	Killed by rancher as a stock killer.	F	Rancho La Cieneguita, San Javier	?
1998	Trapper. Pers. comm. Hide observed in Hermosillo.	?	San Javier	Sinaloan thornscrub
1998	Trapper. Pers. comm. Hide observed in Hermosillo.	?	San Javier	Sinaloan thornscrub
1998	Fide cattle association official; owner afraid to show hide.	F	Rancho Las Norias, Navajoa	?
1997	Killed by lion hunter as stock killer. Pers. comm., photograph.	F	Rancho La Poza, Huasabas	Sinaloan thornscrub?
1997	Houndsman on guided hunt.	?	Rancho El Rodeo, Baviacora?	Madrean evergreen woodland/Sinaloan thornscrub
05/1997	Killed by rancher as stock killer. Pers. comm., photographs.	M	Ejido La Cebadilla, Sahuaripa	Sinaloan thornscrub
1997	Killed by rancher as stock killer. Pers. comm.	F	Rancho La Montosa, Baviacora	Madrean evergreen woodland
1996–1997	Killed by lion hunter as stock killer. Pers. comm.	M	Sierra de los Chinos, Sahuaripa	Sinaloan thornscrub

Date	Collector or Reporter	Sex	Location/Municipo	Biotic Community[1]
1994–1997	Predator hunter. Pers. comm. Skin of one male photographed.	2 M + 1 F + 2 cubs	San Javier	Sinaloan thornscrub
1986–1997	Killed by rancher as stock killer. Pers. comm.	5 M + 1 F	Rancho El Naranjo–El Maquipo, Quiriego	Sinaloan deciduous forest
1996	Killed by lion hunter as stock killer. Pers. comm., photograph.	F	Divisideros/Huasabas	Sinaloan thornscrub
1995	Killed by lion hunter as stock killer. Pers. comm., photograph.	F	Sierra de los Chinos, Sahuaripa	Sinaloan thornscrub
1995	Killed by ranchmen as stock killer.	M	Lampazos/Badesi, Sahuaripa	?
1994–1995	*Fide* restaurant owner in Yecora.	?	Near La Columbina, Yecora	Sinaloan thornscrub
1994	Trapper. Pers. comm. Hide observed in Hermosillo, photograph.	M	E of Tonichi, Tonichi	Sinaloan thornscrub
1994	Lion hunter. Hide observed at owner's house.	M	Rancho Los Taraices, Rayon	Sinaloan thornscrub
1994	Killed by lion hunter as stock killer. Pers. comm., photograph.	M	Rancho San Vicente, Quieriego	Sinaloan deciduous forest
05/1994	*Fide* Carlos Valdes and nine others.	?	Yabaros-Morocarit area, Huatabampo	Mangrove swamps?
1993	Circumstances unknown. Photographs.	M	Cervantes, Tonichi	?
1993	Taken by rancher as stock killer. Pers. comm., photograph.	M	Near Badesi, Sahuaripa/ Granados	Sinaloan thornscrub
1992–1993	Taken by rancher as livestock killer. Pers. comm.	?	San Pedro de la Cueva	Sinaloan thornscrub
1992	Stock killer. Saw skin and photographs.	F	Near Suaqui, San Pedro de la Cueva	Sinaloan thornscrub
1992	Taken by rancher as stock killer.	M	W of Lampazos, Sahuaripa/Tonichi	Sinaloan thornscrub
12/1989	Predator hunter Frank Tapias, taken as stock killer.	F	Pueblo de Alamos, Ures	Sinaloan thornscrub
1989	Lion hunter. Pers. comm.	?	Arizpe?	?
1988–1989	Alejandro Arias. Taken in winter. Photograph.	M	Sierra Bacatete, Guaymas	Sinaloan thornscrub
1970–1980	Rancher. Trapped.	3 M + 4 F	Sierra Bacatete, Guaymas	Sinaloan thornscrub
1975	Rancher. Pers. comm., photograph.	M	Cerro Gordo near Matape, Villa Pesqueira	Madrean evergreen woodland?
1970–1971	Taken in winter by Adolfo Barragan-López. Photograph.	M	Mts. 40–50 km NE of Restaurante El Chino, on Mexico Hwy 15, Carbo	Sinaloan thornscrub
1967–1969	Sr. Mercer? Story related by niece of Adolfo Barragan-López.	?	Rancho Tabiquito 50–65 km SW of Restaurante El Chino, Hermosillo	Sinaloan thornscrub?
1965	Killed. Photographs of both animals seen.	F + cub	Rancho La Sierrita, Alamos	Sinaloan deciduous forest?
1940–1965	Ranch owner issued and paid depredation permits.	13?	Rancho Cervantes, Tonichi	?
ca. 1960	Found dead off coast in Gulf of California.	?	Near Puerto Libertad, Pitiquito	Sonoran desertscrub
1955	Killed by Dick Woodell. Boone and Crockett Club Record Book 1981.	M	Sierra Bacatete, Guaymas?	Sinaloan thornscrub
1952	Trapped by rancher as stock killer. Pers. comm.	?	Rancho Santa Margarita, Guaymas	Sinaloan thornscrub

Table 2. Jaguars reportedly killed or captured in Sonora, 1900–2000 (continued).

Date	Collector or Reporter	Sex	Location/Municipo	Biotic Community[1]
1950–1951	Lion hunter. Pers. comm.	?	Rancho El Carrizal Quemado, Granados	?
1950	Unknown. Skull in Los Angeles Co. Museum.	F	Rancho Guirocoba, Alamos	Sinaloan deciduous forest
1946–1950	Dale Lee et al. Dale Lee tapes *fide* Neil Carmony.	M	E of Río Yaqui near Soyopa, Soyopa	Sinaloan thornscrub
ca. 1940	Lee Woodell. Mounted specimens in American Museum of Natural History, photographs.	M + 2 F	25 km SE Moreno Sta., Guaymas	Sinaloan thornscrub
before 1939	Charlie Ren. O'Connor 1964.	M	Puerto Libertad, Pitiquito	Sonoran desertscrub
before 1939	Manual Parades. O'Connor 1964.	M	Sierra Cucurpe, Cucurpe	Madrean evergreen woodland
before 1939	Unknown. O'Connor 1964.	?	Sierra Azul, Nogales	Madrean evergreen woodland
before 1939	Unknown. O'Connor 1939; see also F. Hibben *in* Boone and Crockett Club 1981.	?	Sierra Picu, Hermosillo	Sonoran desertscrub
1937	Three Americans from Cleveland. O'Connor 1939.	F + 2 cubs	Río Yaqui, Soyopa?	Sinaloan thornscrub
1936	Unknown vaquero. O'Connor 1939.		Sierra Los Mochis, Hermosillo	Sonoran desertscrub
ca. 1936	Dale Lee et al. McCurdy 1979.	3?	E of Tepache, Sauaripa	Sinaloan thornscrub
1935–1936	Dale Lee et al. McCurdy 1979.	1?	E of junction of Rios Aros and Bavispe, Sahuaripa	Sinaloan thornscrub
11/1935	Mother killed and three-month-old cub captured by Dale Lee et al. McCurdy 1979.	F + 1 cub	E of Ríos Aros and Bavispe, Sahuaripa	Sinaloan thornscrub
summer 1935	Dale Lee et al. McCurdy 1979.	2 F + 1 cub	E of Divisideros; E of Ríos Aros and Granados, Sahuaripa	Sinaloan thornscrub
1935?	"American hunters." O'Connor 1939.	6?	Near Soyopa, Soyopa	Sinaloan thornscrub
1934–1935?	Ranchman. O'Connor 1939.	M	Central part of Río Yaqui, Soyopa	Sinaloan thornscrub
1934	Frank Hibben. Boone and Crockett Record Book 1981	M	Novillo Dam area, San Pedro de la Cueva	Sinaloan thornscrub
ca. 1933	Mr. Obermuller (owner?). Burt (1938) saw skin.	?	Mts. near Alamos, Alamos	Sinaloan deciduous forest
ca. 1932	Mr. Kibbe (owner). Burt 1938 *fide* C. H. Lamb.	?	Mts. 24 km W of Rancho El Alamo, Cerro La Campana or Cerro Santa Teresa, Tubatama	Sonoran desertscrub
1909	Skull no. 8027 in Harvard Museum of Comparative Zoology, Nelson and Goldman 1933.	M?	W side of Sierra Madre directly W of Casas Grandes, Chihuahua	Madrean evergreen woodland?

1. Biotic communities from Brown (1994).

Table 3. Jaguars reportedly killed in Chihuahua, 1900–2000.

Date	Collector or Reporter	Sex	Location/Municipo	Biotic Community[1]
1994	Predator trapper. Pers. comm., photograph.	M	100 km N of Cuauhtémoc at base of Sierra del Nido	Madrean evergreen woodland
1991	Predator trapper. Pers. comm., photograph.	M	25 km NE of Cuauhtemoc	Madrean evergreen woodland
before 1990	Tarahumara Indians. Sergio Alvarez, pers. comm.	?	Guadalupe y Calvo vicinity	Sinaloan deciduous forest
1989	Predator trapper, pers. comm. Hide at University of Chihuahua.	M	Rancho Cuervo SW of Janos	?
1988	Predator trapper. Pers. comm.	M	22 km S of Cuauhtémoc	Madrean evergreen woodland
1957	Recovered by L. R. Commissaris. University of Arizona mammal collection.	M?	5 km S Republica, NW of Batopilas, at 3800 ft	Madrean evergreen woodland

1. Biotic communities from Brown (1994).

Plate 1. Jaguar photographed on March 7, 1996, by Warner Glenn in the Peloncillo Mountains, Arizona.

Plate 2. The jaguar tracked by Warner Glenn in the Peloncillo Mountains, March 7, 1996.

Plate 3. Camtracker portrait of a jaguar in east-central Sonora, Mexico.

Plate 4. Jaguar in native tropical semi-evergreen forest at the Tuxtla-Gutiérrez Nature Area, Chiapas, Mexico.

Plate 5. Portrait of a few-week-old blue-eyed jaguar cub.
Photograph by Louella Brown.

I

Natural History

The leopard is found on the western slope of the Baboquivaris
and the low ranges of mountains to the west, near the Mexican
line. He is a more compact built animal than the lion, and fully as
heavy. The Papago and Yaqui Indians say he is much more to be
feared than the lion. He is beautifully marked, and his skin
commands a high price, both here and in Sonora, being in demand
among the Mexican vaqueros for leggings and saddle trimmings.
"The Fauna of Arizona," Mining and Scientific Press
(March 3, 1883)

Among American cats, the jaguar would seem to be unmistakable.
Such is not the case, however. Ocelots, bobcats, and even mountain
lions—especially young animals—can and have been mistaken for jaguars.
That most people *want* to see a jaguar greatly increases the incidence of
misidentification, and normally reliable people have made jaguars out of
large dogs (especially yellow or black Labrador retrievers) and even house
cats and coatis. Such observations are based on self-induced hysteria because a jaguar is easily identifiable in even the dimmest light. A more reasonable error, one made even by experienced observers, is to misjudge the
jaguar's size. With a great head, thick chest, heavy-set body, short powerful
limbs, and large paws, a male jaguar, especially, appears larger than it actually is. In reality, the height of most jaguars is between 27 and 30 in (68
and 76 cm), which is approximately the same height as an adult mountain
lion.

Physical Description

The eyes of jaguars, always impressive, have round pupils and irises
that range in color from golden to reddish yellow. Very young cubs,

Figure 3. Female jaguar killed near Arivaca, Arizona, in 1949. The deer are buck Coues white-tailed deer. The participants are (left to right): game ranger Pete Peterson, David Karam, Walter Noon Jr., and Walter Noon. Photograph courtesy of Sewell Goodwin and Jerry Wager.

however, have blue eyes. The jaguar's dorsal background color ranges from a pale gray through buffy yellow to a golden orange. An overall orange-buff coat is the most common, with animals in nonforested areas tending to have slightly lighter pelage. The characteristic spots, while small and solid on the head and shoulders, typically take the form of broken rings, or rosettes, on the back and flanks, each rosette encircling an area of tawny buff containing one, two, or, rarely, three dots. Other spots form an irregular line along the back, and the markings on the shoulders tend to be larger than those on the neck, head, and legs. All of the underparts are white, and except for a series of black bars on the chest, are marked with black splotches that are usually larger than those on the orange-colored upper portions. The inside of the ears, lower muzzle, jaw, throat, and underbelly are white or pale gray, as is the inside of the legs. Described as beautiful and striking, the jaguar's pelage can be cryptically concealing. When lying motionless under the dappled light provided by even the sparsest of cover, the jaguar blends in as well as any forest mammal (Figure 3).

The tail is relatively short—between 17.0 and 29.5 in (43 and 75 cm) long and less than half of the length of the cat's head and body. This is pro-

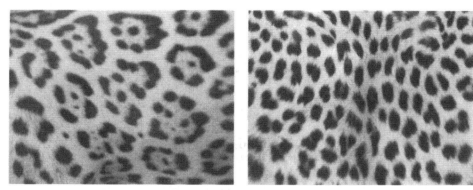

Figure 4. Spotting pattern on a jaguar's pelt (left) compared to an African leopard's (right).

portionately shorter than either an Asian or African leopard's or a mountain lion's tail, which ranges in adult animals from 23.5 to 39.5 in (60 to 100 cm) in the former and from 25 to 38 in (63.5 to 96.5 cm) in the latter, thus accounting for more than half of each animal's total length. The jaguar's tail is also dorsally tawny buff for two-thirds of its length, with the last third being white with solid black spots, so formed as to give the tail's tip a ringed or barred appearance. The jaguar can also be further differentiated from the Old World leopard by the jaguar's shorter tail, barred chest, and the presence of solid dots *within* the broken rosettes (Figure 4).

With the exception of captive animals, which are commonly bred in zoos, black or melanistic jaguars have never been documented north of Mexico's Isthmus of Tehuantepec. This color phase, while comprising up to 6 percent of the population in parts of South America, is virtually unknown in wild populations residing in the subtropical and temperate regions of North America. The northernmost naturally occurring black jaguars that we are aware of are from tropical evergreen forests in Chiapas, Mexico, and in Belize (Figure 5). Even in these melanistic individuals, the darker spots are visible through a somewhat lighter background, which is usually more of a charcoal or dark chocolate color than black. According to genetic studies, these so-called black jaguars are the result of a dominant allele in a particular gene, unlike the recessive allele that results in some Asian leopards becoming black panthers.

Albino jaguars are even rarer. The only literature reference we have come across is one from Paraguay reported by the famous biogeographer-explorer Alexander von Humboldt (1853). Nor are we aware of any small-spotted jaguars, or *tigre pinta menudas,* occurring in the American South-

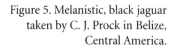

Figure 5. Melanistic, black jaguar taken by C. J. Prock in Belize, Central America.

west or Mexico. These peculiarly marked animals, with small, often broken, rosettes that may or may not contain spots, have only been reported from South America. All of the hides and animals we have examined are typical *tigres mariposas*, or animals having large rosettes with one or more smaller spots (Figure 6). No two jaguars have the exact same coloration or are marked exactly alike. Nor are both sides of the same animal perfectly matched. Thus, individual animals can be identified solely on the basis of their markings.

Although there is much color variation between individual jaguars and fading makes comparison difficult, we can usually differentiate a borderland jaguar hide from one taken farther south. The undersides of Arizona specimens, in particular, usually appear more whitish gray, and the orange background is less rich when compared to more tropical animals. The hair, especially on jaguars taken during the winter months, is measurably longer in most borderland jaguars, and the animals do not appear as sleek as the shorter-haired cats in the tropics. Also, at least some jaguars from Tamaulipas appear to us as more yellowish than most Southwestern cats. But for every sure bet there is an exception, and the above statements are only generalities.

Jaguars have the strongest teeth and jaws of any American cat, and their skulls are more massive and heavy-set than even those of mountain

Figure 6. Mounted jaguar showing camouflage pattern of pelage on leaf litter in oak woodland.

lions. Their large canines are particularly impressive, and the jaguar's jaws are superbly adapted for crushing bones, turtle carapaces, and armadillo shells. Harley Shaw (1983) once observed a drugged captive jaguar crush a veterinarian's 0.5-in (1.3-cm) steel oral speculum merely by closing its jaws together. Sharp, rearward-facing papillae on the tongue facilitate licking any residual meat and marrow from the bones as well as grooming the animal's fur. Like all cats, the jaguar's dental formula is:

$$\frac{3 \text{ incisors } 1 \text{ canine } 3 \text{ premolars } 1 \text{ molar}}{3 \text{ incisors } 1 \text{ canine } 2 \text{ premolars } 1 \text{ molar}}$$

Jaguar skulls can be quickly differentiated from those of mountain lions by examining the skull's palatial foramen. The forward portion of the jaguar's opening has a distinctive fingerlike projection that is lacking in the mountain lion's U-shaped anterior foramen (Figure 7). There are other skull differences, including a concave sweep toward the rear part of the top of the jaguar's skull as opposed to the dorsally convex skull of the mountain lion. Adult jaguar skulls exceed 6 in (15 cm) in width and are wider than those of most Southwestern mountain lions. The jaguar's canine teeth are also larger, and the upper canine will be more than 0.7 in (1.8 cm) wide. These teeth in Southwestern mountain lions usually do not

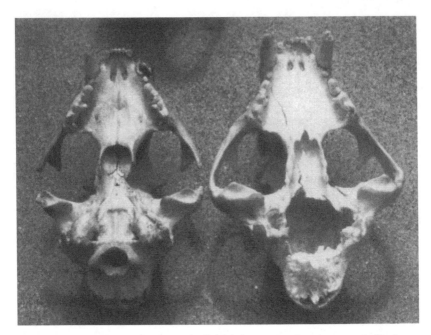

Figure 7. Ventral view of a jaguar skull (right) compared to a mountain lion's (left). Note the fingerlike projection on the anterior portion of the jaguar skull's palatial foramen.

exceed 0.6 in (1.5 cm) in width. Unlike bears and many other mammals, the actual age of these large cats cannot be precisely determined by counting the annuli, or rings, in a tooth's dental cementum. As is the case with mountain lions, however, jaguars can be divided into age classes on the basis of tooth eruption, tooth wear, the length of the cementum ridge from the jaw or skull, and the degree of yellowing (Figure 8). These characters, along with such skull characteristics as the amount of suture closure and sagittal crest development, allow for these cats to be divided into five categories: cub (less than six months old), yearling (six to eighteen months), young mature (eighteen months to three years), prime mature (three to eight years), and old (more than eight years) (Shaw 1983).

Weights and Measurements

When Dale Lee told Jack O'Connor that male jaguars in northwestern Mexico only average about 120 lb (54.5 kg) and females about 80 lb (36 kg), he was pretty much on the mark. Dale's maximum weight for a

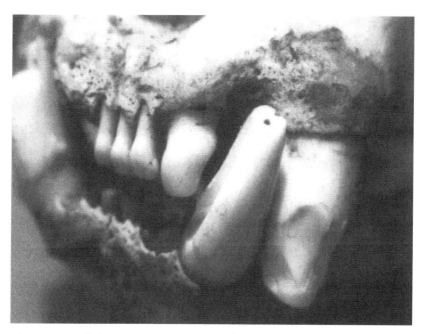

Figure 8. Dental characteristics of an old jaguar. Note the wear on the teeth.

male jaguar was 162 lb (73.5 kg) and his largest female was said to be 90 lb (41 kg). Borderland jaguars are indeed small when compared to their brethren in South America, where a large male may weigh as much as 265 lb (120 kg) and weights exceeding 300 lb (136 kg) have even been reported. The largest jaguar ever measured, a bruiser from Brazil, was more than 9 ft long (109 in, 277 cm) from the tip of his nose to the tip of his tail. But such animals are exceptional, even in South America. In Venezuela adult male jaguars average a little less than 220 lb (100 kg) and females just under 125 lb (57 kg).

Jaguars in Central America and in southern Mexico are much smaller, so much so that Ernest Thompson Seton (1929) termed them "dwarfs." The weights of five female jaguars on the Chamela-Cuixmala Biosphere Reserve in western Mexico, for example, ranged from 77 to 121 lb (35 to 55 kg). It appears that, unlike some other animals, the weights of jaguars may be less a function of latitude and habitat type than the size and abundance of available prey species.

Only a few weights from Southwestern jaguars are available, but these tend to support Jack O'Connor's (1939) statements that, although heavier muscled and possessing a larger, more substantial skull, these jaguars approximate Arizona mountain lions in size. According to Harley Shaw, who conducted research for the Arizona Game and Fish Department, adult male mountain lions in central Arizona average about 137 lb (62 kg), females about 93 lb (42 kg). The dead weight of an adult male jaguar from the Dos Cabezas Mountains in Arizona reportedly was 138 lb (63 kg), and two males, both taken just west of Nogales, Arizona, weighed 88 and 130 lb (40 and 59 kg) with their heart, lungs, and intestines removed (Table 4). If these parts represented 24 percent of the animal's whole weight (as was the case for a female jaguar killed in Arizona's White Mountains that was weighed both whole and dressed), these jaguars would have weighed 116 and 171 lb, respectively, giving an average weight of 143.5 lb (65 kg) for the three males actually weighed on scales. (The female referred to above was full of elk carrion, however, and a more accurate percentage loss for dressed weights is probably closer to 20 percent, making the respective weights of the two males 110 and 163 lb [50 and 74 kg].) Female jaguars are smaller, of course. The two whole weights available for Arizona are 105 and 110 lb (48 and 50 kg; Table 4). This average weight of 107.5 lb (49 kg) is approximately 75 percent of the mean weight of the males.

Other measurements of Southwestern jaguars are equally difficult to come by. Too often the stated measurements are made *after* the hide is removed and subjected to stretching and distortion. For this reason and because of a lack of other corroborating measurements, the total lengths of an Arizona jaguar measured at 119 in (302 cm; in 1902) and another at 93 in (236 cm; in 1912) are disregarded as probable exaggerations (Table 1). Nonetheless, the few measurements available from museum specimens and other reliable sources support the contention that jaguars of the American Southwest, although small compared to their South American brethren, are as large as or larger than any in North America. The Arizona lengths range from 70.0 to 84.4 in (178 to 214 cm), which is larger than five jaguars from Jalisco, Mexico, which ranged only from 43.7 to 72.8 in (111 to 185 cm) in length (Table 5) and the mean length of two males from south Sinaloa, which was less than 69 in (175 cm).

At least some borderland jaguars are large if only by North American standards. The male jaguars taken by U.S. predator control agents in Arizona in 1924 and 1926 are still among the largest ever recorded in North America, according to both Boone and Crockett and Safari Club International record books (Table 4). The 1924 animal, in addition to being the type specimen for the *arizonensis* race, or subspecies, is especially impressive and makes the point that trophy jaguars can be found almost any-

Table 4. Measurements of Southwest borderland jaguars (ordered according to size).

Locale	Year	Sex	Dressed Weight (lb)[1]	Actual Weight (lb)[1]	Total Length (in)[2]	Body Length (in)[2]	B&C Score (in)[2,3]
Cibecue, AZ[4]	1924	M			84.4	58.5	18-5/16
Patagonia, AZ	1926	M					18-3/16
Sahuaripa, SO	1994	M					18
Sahuaripa, SO[5]	1998	M			84.0	58.2	
Guaymas, SO	1940	M					17-14/16
Patagonia, AZ	1926	?					17-8/16
Sahuaripa, SO	2000	M			82.0	60.0	
Sierra Madre, SO	1909	M					17-1/16
Helvetia, AZ	1917	M					16-14/16
Central Sonora	1934	M?					16-14/16
Fort Apache, AZ	1964	M					16-11/16
Sahuaripa, SO	1993	M			79.3	55.8	
Sierra Bacatete, SO	1955	M?					16-11/16
Quiriego, SO	1994	M			73.7	51.4	
Patagonia, AZ	1971	M	130	171[6]	72		
Dos Cabezas, AZ	1986	M	105[6]	138			
Benson, AZ	1961	M			75		16-2/16
Patagonia, AZ	1965	M	88	116[6]	70		15-6/16
Arivaca, AZ	1949	F	84[6]	110	74		
Big Lake, AZ	1961	F	78	105			15-1/16
Guaymas, SO	1940	F			76.7	54.3	14-13/16
Helvetia, AZ	1919	F					14-10/16
Sahuaripa, SO	1999	F			70.8	48.2	14-7/16
Sahuaripa, SO	1995	F					14-3/16
Guaymas, SO	1940	F			67.8	46.8	13-8/16

1. To convert pounds to kilograms, multiply by 0.454.
2. To convert inches to centimeters, multiply by 2.54.
3. Greatest length of skull plus greatest width as taken from *Arizona Wildlife Trophies Book* and the *Boone and Crockett Records Book of North American Big Game*.
4. Hind foot measured 9.1 in.
5. Ear measured 2.0 in.
6. Calculated weight.

where. It is also interesting that the two largest specimens listed in Table 4 were all taken prior to 1930, indicating that there may once have been a general cline in jaguar size in North America, with the largest animals tending to come from the animal's northern limits in Arizona.

Some indications of the relative size of Southwestern jaguars can be obtained from the skull measurements presented in Tables 4, 5, and 6. These scores, obtained from several sources including the trophy books of the Arizona Wildlife Federation and the Boone and Crockett Club, include

Table 5. Measurements of jaguars taken by J. H. Batty from the Pacific Coast of Mexico.

Locale	Year	Sex	Total Length (in)[1]	Body Length (in)[1]	Hind Foot (in)[1]	Ear (in)[1]	B&C Score (in)[1,2]
Escuinapa, Sinaloa	1901	M	68	43.5	9	3.4	15
Escuinapa, Sinaloa	1905–1906	M	69.5	45.5	9	3.3	
Escuinapa, Sinaloa	1905–1906	F					15-11/16
Escuinapa, Sinaloa	1905–1906	immature F					15-11/16
Escuinapa, Sinaloa	1905–1906	F					14
Escuinapa, Sinaloa	1905–1906	F					13

1. To convert inches to centimeters, multiply by 2.54.
2. Boone and Crockett score; total length plus total width.

measurements from most borderland jaguar museum specimens. These measurements are useful in determining the relative size of North American jaguars because they are merely the sums of the skull's greatest length and breadth (usually the width at the skull's zygomatic arches; Figure 7), and are not subject to shrinkage or stretching. These skull measurements indicate that borderland jaguars are not only significantly smaller than any population in South America (which may have Boone and Crockett scores exceeding 20 in [50.8 cm]), but that specimens from the Southwest are close to the size of analogous populations in Texas and northeastern Mexico (Table 6). Ten Boone and Crockett jaguars from Arizona and Sonora averaged 16.7 in (42 cm); fifteen jaguars from Texas and northeastern Mexico averaged 16.6 in (42 cm). The relatively few available jaguar weights from Texas and northeastern Mexico also indicate that northeastern Mexican jaguars are comparable to Southwestern jaguars in size (see Tables 4 and 6).

Borderland jaguars appear to be measurably larger than those found immediately to the south in the Mexican states of Sinaloa and Nayarit (Tables 4 and 5). This comparison is also supported by Boone and Crockett scores, which although probably favoring large males, are roughly comparable between regions. Although the scores of the ten animals from Arizona and Sonora averaged 16.7 in (42 cm), the mean of twenty-one jaguars from Sinaloa, Nayarit, and Jalisco was only 16.2 in (41 cm). Jaguars from southern Mexico south of the Isthmus of Tehuantepec and from Central America also tend to be on the small side. This is of some interest in that the two smallest entries in the Arizona Wildlife Federation's jaguar records, neither of which is included here, were taken on hunts guided by

5

Table 6. Measurements of jaguars from Texas and northeastern Mexico.

Locale	Year	Sex	Dressed Weight (lb)[1]	Actual Weight (lb)[1]	Total Length (in)[2]	Body Length (in)[2]	B&C Score (in)[1,3]
San Andres Tuxla, Veracruz	1894	M?					17-7/8
Mills Co., TX	1903	M	106[4]	140	78		17-1/8
Tampico, Veracruz	1910	M	134[4]	176	78.5	57.5	
San Benitio Co., TX	1946	M		159			

1. To convert pounds to kilograms, multiply by 0.454.
2. To convert inches to centimeters, multiply by 2.54.
3. Boone and Crockett score; total length of skull plus total width.
4. Calculated weight.

an individual who had been convicted of releasing mountain lions for clients in Idaho and who kept live jaguars in his hunting camp in British Honduras.

Vocalizations

One of the most distinctive features separating the jaguar from other New World cats is its penchant for calling as a means of communicating. Although jaguars possess a repertoire of calls, including a variety of snarls and growls, the commonly termed "roars" are more aptly described as a series of three to fifty or more short, hoarse coughs or grunts, an *uh, uh, uh, uh* growing faster and more repetitive until, after several repetitions, the final *uh*s grow so faint as to be inaudible. According to experienced observers, jaguars appear to grunt with their heads held close to the ground, and the depth of tone can be used to distinguish the coughs of males from females as well as the coughs of adults from younger animals. These calls, which are ventriloquial in nature and hard to locate, are said to be most commonly heard during the monsoon breeding season. If so, this is because the calls are used to announce the animal's presence and possibly its reproductive condition. The amount of calling may also reflect jaguar density, the grunts being given more frequently in unexploited habitats than in disturbed areas. Interestingly, we know of no one who has reported hearing these calls in Arizona. Whether this is due to the low density of jaguars, the rarity of such activity, or the unfamiliarity of the observers with the calls is a matter for conjecture.

Sign

In addition to calling, male jaguars designate their home range boundaries by scratching on trees, spraying urine on bushes, and urinating and rolling in soft vegetation or bedding areas. Mature male jaguars may also use their hind legs to make a scrape or a scratch in loose earth, which typically measures about 4 in (10 cm) wide by 12.0–14.5 in (30–37 cm) long. Jaguar scrapes, which sometimes contain feces and urine, are relatively uncommon, however, and are thought to be restricted to areas having dense populations. Nowhere do jaguars make scrapes as frequently as mountain lions, and because both cats share the same range in much of the border country, it is best to assume that a scrape is made by a lion rather than a jaguar, unless other corroborating sign is present. Lion scratches are typically 6–12 in (15–30 cm) long, have a mound of debris at the posterior end, and may or may not be topped by feces. These scratches are usually found along ridges, in saddles, and along major drainages—often under large trees. Mountain lions use these scratches to mark their home range, and they are found most often where the ranges of two or more mountain lions come together.

Jaguars are much more prone than mountain lions to make mounds, large piles of leaves and debris. Lion mounds, when found, are usually 2–3 ft (0.6–0.9 m) in diameter and 12–18 in (30–46 cm) high. Jaguar mounds are typically larger, being about 4–5 ft (1.2–1.5 m) in diameter and looking like a buried kill. As with scrapes, the mound may or may not have feces present.

Tracks

Jaguar tracks are distinctive in their roundness, both in the pad and in the four toes that touch the ground (Figure 9). The jaguar's tracks are also larger than most mountain lions'. The front tracks usually measure between 3.5 and 5.0 in (9 and 13 cm) wide and the rear tracks being between 3 and 4 in (7.6 and 10.2 cm) wide, with a 20-in (50-cm) stride between tracks. The feet of both cat species grow rapidly between three and four years of age, the male's faster than the female's. Thus, the tracks of male jaguars less than two years old are sometimes difficult to differentiate from an adult female's. Males older than three years have tracks larger than any female's and tend to have a rounder imprint and rounder toes. The

Figure 9. Jaguar tracks. Note the rounder and proportionally larger toes.

Figure 10. Mountain lion tracks. Note the deeply three-lobed heel.

toes of the mountain lion are more elongated than those of either sex of jaguar.

The front tracks of both jaguars and mountain lions are larger and rounder than the rear tracks, but it is the heel prints that possess the most diagnostic features, along with making a cleaner, or more visible, track. The rear tracks are also often superimposed wholly or partially upon the front track, so that the width of the heel pad is the most useful measurement for determining both the species and sex of the individual animal involved. Mature male lions in southern Arizona have hind-foot pad measurements ranging from 2.0 to 2.2 in (5.1 to 5.6 cm) in width. The hind-foot pad of mature females lions measures between 1.6 and 2.0 in (4.1 and 5.1 cm). Hind-foot pad widths of 1.5 in (3.8 cm) or less are young animals and tracks less than 1.3 in (3.3 cm) are a bobcat, or, if one is in Sonora, possibly an ocelot. The range of jaguar hind-foot pad widths in Sonora ranged from 2.3 to 3.5 in (5.8 to 8.9 cm) for males and from 2.0 to 2.5 in (5.1 to 6.4 cm) for females.

Size, however, is not necessary the best means of differentiating cat tracks. Tracking is an art as much as a science, and with a little experience, jaguar prints can be distinguished from lion prints by the lion's relatively smaller pads and more elongated toes. The jaguar paw print also has a relatively large central lobe and rounder toes, and although the heel pads of female and young male jaguars are faintly indented, the heel pads of an adult male jaguar are distinctly squared off. All lion tracks, where the heel is showing, display a distinctive three-lobed heel print (Figure 10).

A houndsman named Jack Childs (1998) developed a method to differentiate jaguar tracks from mountain lion tracks. He found that the print of a jaguar's hind-foot pad accounted for an average of 14 percent more of the total track size than a mountain lion's hind pad, and that the area of the jaguar's hind-foot pad took up more than 40 percent of the print's total area as opposed to the mountain lion's hind pad, which accounted for from 28.0 to 38.5 percent of the track area. The species in question can thus be determined by using the following formula.

$$hind\ foot\ (percent) = \frac{(width\ of\ pad \times length\ of\ pad)}{(width\ of\ track \times length\ of\ track)}$$

Using an actual example of a North American jaguar, a hind-foot track measuring 2.25 in wide by 2.69 in long had a heel pad print that was 1.94 in wide and 2.00 in long:

$$hind\ foot = \frac{(1.94 \times 2.00)}{(2.25 \times 2.69)} = 64\ percent$$

Conversely, a track measuring 3.00 in wide by 3.13 in long and having a heel pad 1.75 in wide by 1.50 in long turned out to be a mountain lion:

$$hind\ foot = \frac{(1.75 \times 1.50)}{(3.00 \times 3.13)} = 28\ percent$$

We know of no one who can differentiate jaguar scat from that of a mountain lion's without accompanying tracks. Nonetheless, droppings of the two species have been successfully separated through DNA analysis. This laboratory procedure is expensive, however, and should only be resorted to in the most unusual of circumstances.

Subspecies

Until the habit of scientific accuracy in observation and record is achieved, and until specimens are preserved and carefully compared, entirely truthful men, at home in the wilderness, will whole-heartedly accept, and repeat as matters of gospel faith, theories which split the grizzly and black bears of each locality in the United States, and the lions and black rhinos of South Africa, or the jaguars and pumas of any portion of South America, into several different species, all with widely different habits.

Theodore Roosevelt (1914) *Through the Brazilian Wilderness*

The concept of dividing species into races or subspecies that are imperfectly or only recently reproductively isolated and that are differentiated on the basis of color, size, or some other physiognomic character has undergone several changes since most mammal subspecies were described during the first half of the twentieth century. During that time, a literal handful of American mammalogists described numerous subspecies, often on the basis of the skull measurements of a relatively few individuals. The jaguar was typical of this procedure. E. A. Mearns (1901) described several subspecies of jaguars on the basis of only a few specimens. Using a larger, but still inadequate sample, this effort was revised by E. W. Nelson and E. A. Goldman (1933) of the U.S. National Museum, who described most of the races of North America's large mammals. Later, R. I. Pocock (1939) recognized five North American subspecies: *P. o. arizonensis,* said to range from Arizona southward to southern Sonora; *P. o. hernandesii,* ranging from southern Sonora southward to the state of Guerrero, Mexico; *P. o. centralis,* which resided from south of the Isthmus of Tehuantepec down through Central America and into Columbia; *P. o. goldmani,* living on the Yucatán Peninsula; and *P. o. veraecrucis,* which once occupied southern Texas and eastern Mexico from Tamaulipas southward to Tabasco (Map 1).

The recognition of these subspecies, although widely repeated, is probably moot in that scientists now have a much better understanding of gene flow among large predatory animals. Not only did a recent analysis of American museum specimens show more variation within the various subspecies than between them, emerging DNA analysis shows only two major regions having recognizably different genetic material: one including all areas north of the Amazon River and another south of the river. Although there is little available information on jaguar dispersal, other large male cats have been known to travel more than 300 mi (480 km) in their search for a mate, and it makes little sense to draw arbitrary lines separating so-called *arizonensis* animals from an adjacent population of *hernandesii.* The same can be said for trying to separate *centralis* from *goldmani* and *hernandesii* and *goldmani* from *veraecrucis.* Nonetheless, because jaguars are absent from Mexico's Central Plateau, the animals inhabiting Mexico's eastern and western coasts may be effectively isolated from each other. It therefore makes sense to continue to treat animals from these two biotic regions as distinct populations.

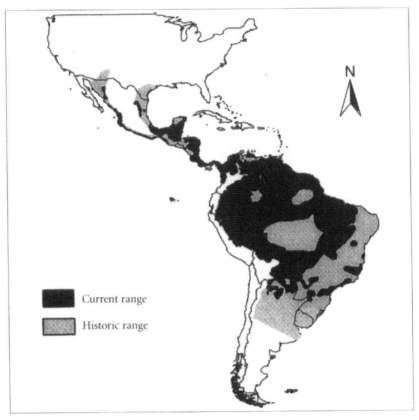

Map 1. Presumed historic and current range of jaguars in the Western Hemisphere.

Fossil Record

But the climate probably was too severe; for the species can be considered only accidental in the United States except in the low forests of southern Texas and the southeast corner of Arizona, where heat, timberland, and abundance of game appear to have given it a permanent footing.

　　　　　Ernest Thompson Seton (1929) *Lives of Game Animals*

Jaguars belong to the subfamily *Panthera*, which includes the African lion *(Panthera leo)*, tiger *(P. tigris)*, and three species of leopards *(P. pardus, Unica uncia,* and *Neofelis nebulosa)*—the so-called roaring cats. Paleontologists believe that the genus originated in the Old World, the ancestor of our present jaguar having evolved somewhere in Eurasia before

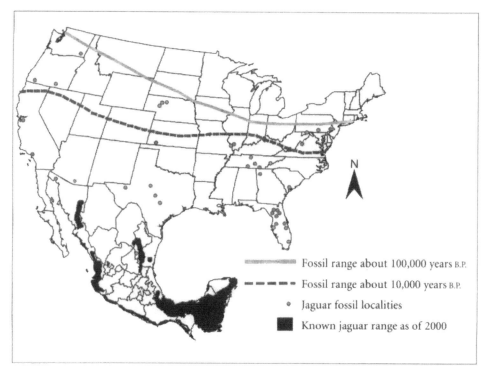

Map 2. Jaguar fossil distribution in North America. Modified from publications by Ron Nowak (1975, 1994), Björn Kürten and Elaine Anderson (1980), and K. L. Seymour (1989).

moving southward into Europe and into North America. Whatever its origins, *Panthera* arrived in North America via Beringia during the Pleistocene era, nearly 2 million years ago, at about the same time as mammoths *(Mammuthus)*, shrub-oxen *(Euceratherium)*, and other taiga-dwelling mammals. By middle Irvingtonian times, about 600,000 years ago, a large race of jaguar, *Panthera onca augusta*, had separated from the leopards, lions, and other members of the genus. This larger version of today's jaguar was by then not only roaming much of North America, it had also begun to invade South America following the formation of the Isthmus of Panama. Fossil remains, not all of which have been validated, place prehistoric jaguars in numerous sites in North America, from as far north as the present states of Washington and Pennsylvania southward to Mexico (Map 2). Pleistocene jaguars have also been found in the Southwest in what are now the states of Texas, New Mexico, Arizona, and Sonora, where they coexisted with mammoths, tapirs, prehistoric peccaries, extinct pronghorns, and ground sloths.

As the Pleistocene advanced and forests gave way to glaciers, grass-lands, and savannas, the forest-dwelling *P. o. augusta* retreated southward and eastward. In the far West, in what is now southern California, jaguar fossils become conspicuously absent during the last 50,000 years, the principal cats in areas such as the La Brea tar pits being a larger version of the African lion *(Panthera leo atrox)* and other grassland-inhabiting felids. Rarely, in fact, have these two species of *Panthera* been found together. Toward the end of the Pleistocene, between 15,000 and 10,000 years ago, North American jaguars had diminished in size, probably due to increasing aridity and a declining size in their prey. That the jaguar is today the New World's biggest cat is an artifact of evolutionary history, with the animal somehow adapting to a smaller and more general prey base than was present when it evolved. This reduction in body mass, concomitant with a shrinkage in distribution, has continued on into recent times. Nonetheless, the jaguar was able to persist in North America, whereas its more open-country relative, *Panthera leo,* became extinct during Holocene times, between 10,000 and 11,000 years ago. Jaguars were even present in Florida a mere 7000–8000 years ago. In this respect, it may be significant that the jaguar and leopard of Africa and Asia are still closely enough related that matings of the two species in zoos have produced hybrids that were fertile to at least the first generation.

Distribution

Few predatory animals are such wanderers as the jaguar, which roams hundreds of miles from its original home, as shown by its occasional appearance within our borders.

E. W. Nelson in Seton (1929)

Jaguars were, and in part remain, widely distributed in the southern portions of the Western Hemisphere from the southwestern United States to southern and eastern Bolivia, extreme western and eastern Paraguay, and the most northern and northeastern parts of Argentina (Map 1). Jaguars were apparently never present in extreme southern South America, and these cats did not historically occur in Chile; west of the eastern escarpments of the Andes Mountains; or in the cold, windswept, and arid portions of Patagonia. According to South American biologists Hoogesteijn and Mondolfi (1993), the jaguar disappeared from Uruguay about 1900 and was extirpated from the open Pampas by 1925. The jaguar has disappeared from many other locales since then, and this species is apparently no longer a breeding animal in either El Salvador or the United States. Much of the jaguar's habitat in Mexico has now been destroyed, as it has in much of Central America. Sizable populations remain, however, in southern Mexico, in the wildest parts of Central America, and in northern South America—particularly in Venezuela, Brazil, Ecuador, and the Guianas, where jaguars are protected in a number of national parks and preserves. The range and size of populations elsewhere in South America are largely unknown (Map 1).

Jaguars in Central America are now restricted to the more remote districts of Panama and Costa Rica, eastern Nicaragua, northern and eastern Honduras, northern Guatemala, and Belize, where thrifty populations remain present. In Mexico, good numbers of jaguars are thought to inhabit parts of Quintana Roo, Campeche, and Chiapas, with other populations likely surviving in the more remote portions of the western states of Oaxaca, Michoacán, Guerrero, Jalisco, Nayarit, and Sinaloa. South and east of the Central Mexican Plateau, jaguars persist only in the undeveloped parts of Yucatán, Tabasco, Veracruz, Tamaulipas, Nuevo León, and possibly San Luis Potosí and Queretaro. Jaguars periodically reported in other Mexican states are more likely to be wanderers than remnants of a relict population.

Plotting the historic distribution of jaguars in the Southwest is no easy matter. Jaguars have been killed as far north as the Grand Canyon in Arizona and in the Datil Mountains in New Mexico (Table 1), and almost every jaguar distribution map ever published includes portions of these two states as part of the animal's historic range. Although there are no "jaguar" place names in Arizona or New Mexico, there are several places in Arizona that contain the word "leopard," "tiger," or *"tigre"* indicating that jaguars may once have occurred there (Table 7). A number of these name-sites are based on reported sightings and other questionable sources, however, and cannot be taken at face value. One of he best early maps was drawn up in 1923 by Ernest Thompson Seton with the assistance of the U.S. Biological Survey (Map 3). This map not only includes portions of Arizona, New Mexico, and Texas as historic jaguar range, it presents a number of dot records for supposed jaguar observations in these states as well as California and Colorado. Even if these observations were valid, one has to ask if these animals represented a breeding population. The answer, at least in the case of the more outlandish records, is probably no. But if not, where was the most northern breeding population? Females have

Map 3. Range of the jaguar in North and Central America. Compiled by E. T. Seton in 1923 with the aid of the U.S. Biological Survey.

reportedly been killed as far north as the Grand Canyon, and there are accounts of hunters taking both young jaguars and jaguars running together as far north as the Mogollon Rim (Maps 4 and 5). The only actual account of jaguar cubs being taken in the American Southwest, however, is limited to a June 1, 1906, *Arizona Daily Star* article in which a female jaguar was reportedly killed in the Chiricahua Mountains and her two cubs are captured and offered for sale:

Table 7. Borderland place names that refer to jaguars.

Place Name	Coordinates	Description
Tiger, Arizona	34°09'N, 112°21'W	Mine, canyon, and former settlement in Bradshaw Mts., Yavapai Co.
Tiger Butte, Arizona	33°56'N, 109°39'W	Butte on White Mountain Apache Indian Reservation, Apache Co.
Leopard Springs, Arizona	33°53'N, 111°07'W	Former name of Mud Springs on Tonto National Forest, Gila Co.
Tiger, Arizona	33°45'N, 113°14'W	Wash and two wells SW of Wickenburg, Maricopa Co.
El Tigre Mine	33°44'N, 113°11'W	Mine site
Tiger, Arizona	32°43'N, 110°41'W	Mountain, mining town, and mine W of Mammoth, Pinal Co.
El Tigre Mine	31°56'N, 109°17'W	Mine shaft in the Chiricahua Mts.
El Tigre, Sonora	30°35'N, 109°13'W	Mine and settlement on W side of Sierra San Diego (Sierra El Tigre)
Sierra El Tigre	30°33'N, 109°15'W	Local name for Sierra San Diego
Cerro Tigre	30°12'N, 110°52'W	Hill W of Sierra Cucurpé
Arroyo del Tigre, Sonora	29°52'N, 109°39'W	Arroyo S of Moctezuma, SO
Rancho Tigre, Sonora	29°35'N, 110°50'W	SW of Rayón
Cerro Tigre, Sonora	28°27'N, 110°05'W	Hill W of Suaqui Grande
Cerro Tigre, Sonora	28°04'N, 110°56'W	Hill, arroyo, and bridge N of Guaymas
Yocorato, Sonora	27°35'N, 108°46'W	E of San Bernardo
Yocojihua, Sonora	26°47'N, 109°01'W	Mayo site S of Alamos
El Tigre, Chihuahua	27°59'N, 108°38'W	Settlement on Arroyo Santismo
Tigrito, Chihuahua	27°37'N, 107°48'W	Site
El Tigre, Chihuahua	26°30'N, 107°42'W	Site near Los Palomas
Questa del Tigre	26°58'N, 108°27'W	Near the head of San Francisco Canyon, which drains into the Río Chiapas near where the borders of Sonora, Sinaloa, and Chihuahua meet

Snarling, fighting and frantic in their efforts to break through the wooden cage . . . two tigers were offered for sale by two Mexicans in Bisbee yesterday. Though only a few weeks old the little tigers are full of life. . . . To capture the pups the Mexicans had to shoot the mother tiger who they discovered guarding her young in a lonely part of the Chiricahua Mountains. . . . Asked what price they would take for the tigers the Mexicans stated that they would sell the two of them for $150 or one for $80.

The next most northern account of cubs is from east-central Sonora (Table 2). No female jaguars are known to have been taken in New Mexico, where a jaguar hasn't been killed since 1909 (Table 1). Jaguar place names are lacking in New Mexico, thus the species was probably always rare in that state and a breeding population there unlikely. Jaguars in the American Southwest were probably limited to sub-Mogollon southeastern Arizona and possibly extreme west-central New Mexico.

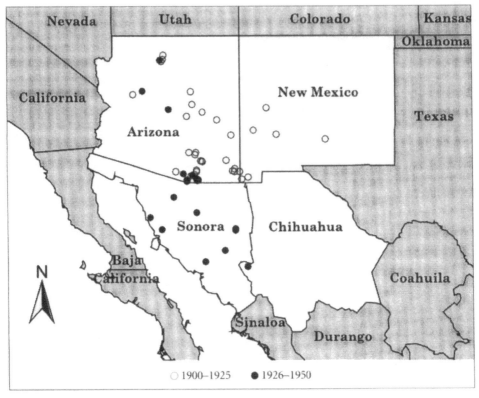

Map 4. Borderland jaguars killed between 1900 and 1950.

The situation in Sonora is more clear-cut. Recent kill records and accounts, with a few exceptions, generally coincide with the identification of "jaguar country" in a hunter's map drawn up by American sportsmen around 1950 (Map 6). Jaguar place names, both in Spanish and Cahita, are also sprinkled throughout eastern and southern Sonora (Table 7). These names, along with recent kill data, show jaguars as living in the more rugged and better watered mountains in the eastern and southern portions of Sonora, with only an occasional animal being killed in the western deserts and along the coast (Table 2, Maps 4 and 5).

During the course of this study, we also obtained six jaguar records from the state of Chihuahua (Figure 11, Table 3). These animals, which were all males taken in Madrean evergreen woodland, are presumably transients from east-central Sonora (Map 5). Based on physiographic and vegetational affinities, however, it is not unlikely that jaguars also live in the *barranca* country in the far southwestern reaches of that state.

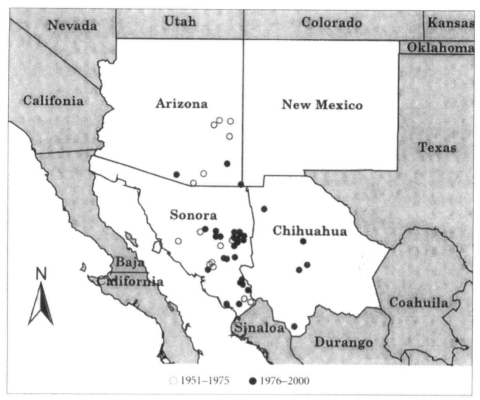

Map 5. Borderland jaguars killed or photographed between 1951 and 2000.

No mention of the jaguar's distribution in the Southwest would be complete without some mention of the cat's former occurrence in Texas. Early reports, including those by Spencer F. Baird (1859) of the U.S. National Museum, described this species as common in southern Texas. Baird stated that jaguars once ranged into central Texas and had been found as far east as the Louisiana border and as far north as the Red River (Map 1). Populations must have declined rapidly after independence in 1845, however, because a male killed in 1879 about 10 mi south of Carrizo Springs in Dimmit County was described as a rare animal even then. Vernon Bailey, in his 1905 biological survey of Texas, went on to report that only a few jaguars had been taken in Texas in the 1880s and 1890s, and that he considered this species as "now extremely rare." Indeed, only six jaguars are known to have been killed in that state in the twentieth century (Table 8), and the species was said to have been extirpated from Texas sometime before 1927. Actually, none of the jaguars taken in Texas during the 1900s

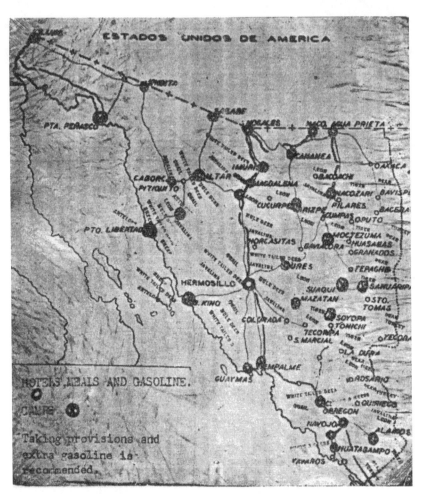

Map 6. Hunter's map of Sonora, Mexico, showing jaguar and other game concentrations circa 1950. Courtesy of the Arizona Historical Society, Tucson.

is known to have been a female, and the species was probably extirpated as a resident animal prior to the turn of the century. Jaguars killed in Texas after that time were almost certainly transients from northern Tamaulipas, where houndsmen such as Roy T. McBride, then a graduate student working on mountain lions, found fair numbers of jaguars in the 1960s. Interestingly, the plotted locales of jaguars killed in Texas were in Tamaulipan semideciduous forest, Tamaulipan thornscrub, and oak-juniper *encinals* with large rivers nearby. Except for an animal taken in Southeastern deciduous and evergreen forest in the Big Thicket, these animals were all killed in biotic communities analogous to those used by jaguars in Arizona

Figure 11. Adult male jaguar trapped by a ranchman northeast of Cuauhtemoc, Chihuahua, in 1991.

and Sonora. That jaguars no longer visit these habitats in Texas is probably due to their absence in northern Tamaulipas as much as to habitat loss. Southern Texas still contains large tracts of Tamaulipan thornscrub and *encinal* woodland, some of which contain high densities of deer and javelina.

In his 1905 monograph on the mammals of Texas, Vernon Bailey published a letter to the U.S. National Museum from the naturalist H. P. Attwater describing the locality where a "fine old male jaguar" was killed near Center City, Mills County, just north of Texas's Colorado River:

> I took particular note of the country around Goldthwaite and in that part where the animal was killed it is rough with rocky ridges which they call 'mountains,' running parallel with the creeks and rivers, with uneven valley lands between the streams and the mountains. There is no tall timber, but the entire country is covered with a thick brush or chaparral, consisting chiefly of shin oak thickets known as the 'shinnery,' also sumac thickets and Spanish oak clumps with live oak trees scattered among them. On the lower flats there are considerable mesquite trees.

Table 8. Jaguars reportedly killed in Texas, 1900—1999.[1]

Date	Collector/Reporter	Sex	Location and Description	Biotic Community[2]
1948	*Federal Register* 1993, 58(69):19218.	?	Kleburg Co.	Tamaulipan thornscrub
30/1/1946	Taken by Arnaldo Martinez as stock killer. Taylor 1947.	M	6 mi SE of San Benito, Cameron Co. 159 lb.	Tamaulipan semideciduous forest
ca. 1912	Unknown. Seton 1929, Taylor 1947.	?	Near Lyford, Willacy Co.	Tamaulipan semideciduous forest
spring 1910	Unknown. *Forest and Stream* 1/7/1911, Seton 1929 *fide* V. Bailey	M	Near London, Kimble Co., near Llano River. "Large."	Balcones encinal woodland
9/3/1903	Mr. Hudson and party; treed while hunting with dogs. Bailey 1905, skin and skull in U.S. National Museum	M	3 mi SW of Center City, Mills Co. 140 lbs.	Balcones encinal woodland
ca. 1900	Unknown. Bailey 1905.	?	S of Jasper along Nueces River near Beaumont, Jasper Co.	Southeastern deciduous and evergreen forest

1. Does not include guided hunts.
2. Biotic communities from Blair (1950) and Brown (1994).

Although the idea of jaguars in the Grand Canyon may seem extreme, there are records of jaguars even farther afield. During the last 150 years, jaguars have been reported from northern New Mexico, Colorado, California, and even Baja California. Several of these reports have been accepted at face value, and all of them need to be addressed.

Northern New Mexico

Coronado, while traveling to the Zuni pueblos in 1540, included both *tigres* and *ounces* among the mammals of the region—a narrative repeated in Whipple's (1856) report to the U.S. Congress on a proposed railroad route along the thirty-fourth parallel. Another northern New Mexico report—a bloody and much-publicized translation by C. B. R. Kennerly—of a Spanish account that was repeated in Vernon Bailey's *Mammals of New Mexico,* describes a *tigre* entering the Convent of San Francisco in Santa Fe on April 10, 1825, and, without provocation, attacking and killing four men before finally being shot through a hole bored in the sacristy door. Perhaps to account for this unusual behavior, Kennerly and Bailey also included the explanation that the animal had been driven into the convent's garden by flood waters from the Rio Grande. But the explanation is moot. The translation is in error. The much publicized event took place at the Convent of San Francisco in Santa Fe, Argentina, *not* New

Mexico, and the flooding river is the Para, *not* the Rio Grande. Even though several authors have attempted to correct this account (e.g., O'Mara 1997), the original translation continues to be reprinted from time to time because it captures the public's imagination.

Another more recent record of a jaguar in northern New Mexico is provided by J. Hill (1942), who reported a jaguar as being killed "some years ago" near Springer in northeastern New Mexico, and that the skin was in the collection of Mr. Waite Phillips. Springer is located in open plains grassland, and the nearby hills are clothed in junipers and piñons where not covered by shrub oaks and montane scrub. Adding to the unlikelihood of this account is that this location is more than 200 mi from the nearest other New Mexico kill—itself, an extreme location in the Datil Mountains (Table 1, Map 4).

Colorado

The literate trapper Rufous B. Sage (1857) reported that in December 1843, while camped at the base of the Rocky Mountains on Soublet's Creek, headwaters of the Platte River, within 30 or 40 mi of Long's Peak, "One of our party encountered a strange looking animal in his excursions, which from his description, must have been of the Leopard family." On the basis of this entry, Ernest Thompson Seton (1920) thought that this record might provide a "new mammal for Colorado." Colorado mammalogist E. R. Warren also considered Sage's report to be a possible jaguar and determined that the encounter took place in November 1843, perhaps in Estes Park, but certainly in the South Platte drainage near Long's Peak. However, another mammalogist, A. R. Armstrong, was reluctant to concede even the barest possibility that this animal was a jaguar, pointing out that this secondhand report could have been an immature mountain lion. Because the particulars of the encounter are not described, another possibility is that the trapper saw a hide or pelt that had been obtained farther south through conquest or trade, as Sage himself stated that "Leopard skins furnish to the natives [Comanches] a favorite material for arrow-cases."

California

Largely on the basis of Native American recollections, a number of early naturalists such as C. H. Merriam, W. D. Strong, and Joseph Grinnell regarded the jaguar as formerly present in the Cuyamaca and other southern California mountain ranges, the last animal being killed "in the [Santa Rosa] mountains along the west side of the Colorado Desert back of Palm Springs about 1860." This last jaguar supposedly met its fate while attacking a Native hunter wearing antlers and a deer skin. ¿Quien sabe? Although accepted by Seton and other wildlife chroniclers, an account of "Grizzly" Adams encountering a family of jaguars on the south side of Tejon Pass in the Tehachapi Mountains about 1855 comes across as so implausible as to be ludicrous (see Hittell 1860).

Baja California

While trapping beavers along the lower Colorado River in the 1820s, James Ohio Pattie (1905) reported that, "We killed some wild geese and pelicans, and likewise an animal not unlike the African leopard, which came into our camp, while we were at work upon the canoe. It was the first that we had ever seen." This site, on an island probably not far from the Colorado River Delta and close to today's Baja California Norte–Sonora boundary, is not that unreasonable a location for a jaguar. Given Pattie's matter-of-fact description, this may be a bona fide observation.

On the contrary, J. Xantus's (1976) account of a Señor Bacca [Baca?] presenting him with a freshly killed and "truly beautiful jaguar skin" in 1858 is not to be believed. Although Xantus accurately describes the skin as yellowish with black rosettes and states that it was killed in the vicinity of silver mines some 40 mi west of San Felipe and 50 mi from San Bartoleme (Vizcaíno) Bay, Xantus's itinerary and descriptions of other encounters in Baja California brand him as a fake. Not only is the timetable of his overland travels totally implausible, but he also claimed to have encountered Papago Indians, armadillos, peccaries, and 6-lb quail with 4.5-ft plumes, not to mention squads of grizzly bears and an abundance of jaguar sign on his Baja California travels. Even allowing for Baron Munchausen–like exaggerations, armadillos and peccaries have never been present in Baja California, nor have the Tohono O'odham Indians.

An account of A. Starker Leopold in his *Wildlife of Mexico,* in which he states: "I recently examined the tanned hide of a jaguar killed in September, 1955, near the southern tip of the Sierra Pedro Martir range, Baja California," is more problematic. To continue Leopold's quote, "This animal, an old male, must have wandered across the whole Sonoran Desert, crossed the Colorado River, and traveled south for 100 miles—a trip of at least 500 miles from regularly occupied jaguar range. Most vagrant jaguars are males, presumably driven from home in territorial disputes with other males. Once on the road, such vagrants seem to adopt travel as a way of life, like itinerant Englishmen." One has to conclude that there is no other ready explanation for this animal's presence so far out of its normal range.

Although some of these reports of jaguars in outlying areas were secondhand, and none was documented by a specimen or a photo, not all of these accounts can be dismissed as merely fraudulent, a case of mistaken identity, or an animal that might have escaped from captivity. One is led to conclude that jaguars may possess an amazing propensity to wander, and that an individual animal might turn up hundreds of miles from where it was born.

Habitats

The big cat is most at home in the tall shady forests along streams and watercourses that transverse the coastal lowlands. . . . They are particularly prone to follow the big rivers on their northern peregrinations—the Brazos, Pecos, Rio Grande, Gila, and Colorado.
A. Starker Leopold (1959) *Wildlife of Mexico*

Jaguar habitat in South and Central America has been described as nearly any tropical forest type including evergreen rain forest, evergreen riparian forest, semi-evergreen forest, and dry deciduous forest. The major requirement appears to be a closed vegetative structure. Open country is usually avoided, be it grassland or desertscrub. For this reason, jaguars are nowhere found much above 8500 ft elevation, and as one ascends the Andes and other mountain ranges, the jaguar becomes rare or absent upon reaching the barren *altiplano* and *puna*. Even in the flooded savannas of Venezuela and Brazil, where jaguars are numerous, these big cats tend to remain close to riverine forests and copses of trees. Given the widespread array of potential vegetation types, it is interesting to note that 83 percent of the jaguars taken in Venezuela (when jaguar hunting was still legal) was reportedly in tropical deciduous forest.

Closer to home, jaguars in Central America and southern Mexico are most abundant in the evergreen and semi-evergreen rain and montane

Figure 12. Tropical deciduous forest at Chamela-Cuixmala Biosphere Reserve in Jalisco, Mexico.

Figure 13. (below)Mangrove swamp in the Marismas Nacionáles near the Nayarit-Sinaloa border.

forests of Belize, Guatemala, Chiapas, and Campeche (see Plate 4). Good populations of these big cats formerly extended northward through the evergreen and semi-evergreen forested uplands and swampy lowlands along the Gulf Coast of Mexico from Campeche to Texas. These populations, where they exist at all, are now much fragmented, as is their former habitat. Other populations of jaguars persist in unknown numbers in tropical deciduous and semideciduous forests, primarily in Yucatán, Quintana Roo, Chiapas, and western Mexico.

Figure 14. Madrean evergreen woodland along the U.S.-Mexico border.

Proceeding up the western coast of Mexico, fair numbers of jaguars can still be found in Guerreran dry forest and other habitats in such relatively undisturbed areas as Chamela-Cuixmala Biosphere Reserve in Jalisco (Figure 12). Indeed, respectable examples of this biotic community can still be found in various parts of western Mexico, and jaguars probably continue to persist in a discontinuous string of tropical deciduous forest from southern Oaxaca northward to southern Sonora. Other important habitats for jaguars in western Mexico, although more so formerly than recently, are the mangrove forests and swamps of the Agua Bravo and Marismas Nacionales straddling the borders of Nayarit and Sinaloa (Figure 13). And, although jaguars are generally absent on the Mexican Plateau, individual cats continue to extend upward from the tropical forests along both Mexican coasts into Madrean evergreen woodlands of oaks, junipers, and pines. These woodlands and forests, while not indicative of jaguars per se, constitute important jaguar foraging locales in the Sierra Madre del Sur, Sierra Madre Oriental, Sierra Madre Occidental, and in other places where these temperate woodlands come into contact with tropical forests inhabited by these big cats.

Madrean evergreen woodland is also an important biotic community for borderland jaguars, accounting for nearly 30 percent of the jaguars killed in this region (Figure 14). This is especially true in Chihuahua and

Figure 15. Ranchmen with a jaguar trailed and killed in snow on Cypress Mountain northwest of Prescott, Arizona, in December 1926. Photograph courtesy of Gary Saunders.

the American Southwest, where more than half of the jaguars taken have been in woodlands of oak and pine or other habitats containing strong elements of this biotic community (Tables 1 and 2). Through the use of camera traps, we have also documented jaguars, including females and cubs, using a mosaic of Madrean woodland and Sinaloan thornscrub. Surprisingly, nearly a fourth of the jaguars taken in Arizona and New Mexico were killed either in montane conifer forest or piñon-juniper woodland (Figure 15). Whether such habitats can be considered "jaguar country" or are merely jaguar foraging areas is unknown. The fact that none of the animals reportedly killed in Sonora or Chihuahua was taken in conifer forest may be due to the absence of ranches visited in this biotic community, as pine forest is found immediately above many of the localities where recently killed jaguars were reported.

Kill locations ranged from as low as 500 ft (150 m) in Sonora to more than 9500 ft (2850 m) elevation in Arizona's White Mountains, thus we have concluded that borderland jaguars are primarily montane animals. The most important biotic community for jaguars in the Southwestern borderlands by far is Sinaloan thornscrub (Figure 16). This biotic community, which occupies the lower bajadas and basins between 1500 and

Figure 16. Sinaloan thornscrub in Sonora, Mexico.

Figure 17. Jaguar habitat in Sinaloan deciduous forest near Cosala, Sinaloa.

Figure 18. Jaguar trapped by predator control agent Russell Culbreath in
semidesert grassland on the White Mountain Apache Indian Reservation.
Photograph courtesy of the U.S. Fish and Wildlife Service.

3100 ft (450 and 930 m) elevation, accounts for nearly 80 percent of the
jaguars killed in Sonora and includes more than 50 percent of the borderland region's total harvest. Largely confined to the state of Sonora, this
unique habitat type is typically sandwiched between the taller Sinaloan
deciduous forest to the south and the more openly structured Sonoran
desertscrub to the north and west. Sinaloan thornscrub is probably the key
habitat type for this most northerly of remaining jaguar populations.
More jaguars were not reported killed in Sinaloan deciduous forest (Figure 17) as a result of us not working farther south in Sonora, where this biotic community becomes the dominant cover and where people are more
afraid to speak to strangers because of the drug traffic. The lack of jaguars
from the Sonoran Desert (about 5 percent of the Southwest total) is real,
however, and is probably a true reflection of the habitat requirements and
preferences of this cat. As stated earlier, jaguars are not desert animals.

A smaller but still significant number of jaguars has been taken in
chaparral and in shrub-invaded semidesert grasslands. This is especially

Figure 19. Potential jaguar habitat in the Coyote Mountains, Arizona. Formerly grassland, this area now has both the aspect and composition of Sinaloan thornscrub, including such characteristic plant species as mesquite (*Prosopis juliflora velutina*), hopbush (*Dodonaea angustifolia*), and kidneywood (*Eysenhardtia orthocarpa*).

true in Arizona, where Sinaloan thornscrub is absent and where semidesert grassland accounts for about 15 percent of the jaguars taken (Table 1, Figure 18). That jaguars use this biotic community is of more than casual interest in that much of Arizona's semidesert grassland has been heavily invaded by species of thornscrub during the last century and now shares many of the physiognomic characteristics and plant species as Sinaloan thornscrub (Figure 19). Ironically, this could be interpreted to mean that Arizona contains better jaguar habitat today than in 1900, when jaguars were presumably more numerous.

The use of riparian areas by jaguars is difficult to determine from kill data alone. Although less than 5 percent of the jaguars were killed along major drainages, and we have concluded that borderland jaguars are primarily montane animals, this species has a definite tendency to prefer the wetter habitats. Inspection of several actual kill sites, coupled with numerous interviews, indicates that many of the jaguars were killed at springs, at stock tanks, near small to medium streams, and in other wetland sites within the mountain range they were using. Major drainages have not been a major habitat type since 1900, which may be influenced by the density of human settlement, a lack of game in most of these areas, and the generally heavily grazed conditions of such sites. The jaguar is, after all, a wilderness animal.

Prey

The word "Jaguar" is said to be the Indian for "Eater of Us."
J. M. Phillips (1913) "Transplanting the Jungle King"

Jaguars are generalists when it comes to their feeding habits, and at least 89 species of animals have been reported as prey items. Prey selection is based on abundance and opportunity as much as size. This tendency to feed on a variety of game may even be greater than is the case with mountain lions, which are so dependent on deer that these animals make up from 40 to 95 percent of their diet. Whether this is also true farther south is less certain, but several studies have shown that the diets of jaguars and pumas always overlap to some degree. Regardless of any preference when it comes to prey selection, both species readily take to killing livestock in areas where either the cats' natural game has been depleted or where calves and yearlings are pastured in rugged, brushy country.

Some indication of the catholic nature of the jaguar's diet can be realized from studies in Brazil, where items in the cats' stomachs have been recorded. In addition to livestock, which are often found in jaguar stomachs if for no other reason than that many of the jaguars killed had been especially sought after as livestock killers, the various food items included tapir, capybara, collared peccary, white-lipped peccary, feral hog, red brocket deer, agouti, coati, puma, anteater (Tamandua), rhea, and grass. A similar variety of somewhat smaller animals were found in Venezuelan jaguar stomachs: collared peccary, caiman, armadillo, iguana, and heron. Even smaller prey animals are the rule in Belize: armadillo, two species of brocket deer, two species of peccary (mostly white-lipped), howler monkey, paca, caiman, iguana, and freshwater turtles.

At Chamela-Cuixmala Biosphere Reserve, which is closed to livestock grazing, jaguars killed only seven species of animals, of which four mammals (white-tailed deer, javelina, armadillo, and coati) provided 98 percent of the biomass taken. Pumas, in contrast, killed sixteen species of prey and

Figure 20. Coues white-tailed deer. These small deer, most weighing less than 100 lb (45 kg), are natural prey of borderland jaguars.

mammals accounted for 94 percent of the biomass. Deer and javelina were the two most preferred items of both cats, each species eating about 5.5 lb of meat at a feeding, or the equivalent of 85 deer per jaguar and 78 deer per puma per year. Along the coast, as in the Agua Brava area of Nayarit, jaguars are more likely to dine on seafood, with fish, turtle, crocodile, and "swamp monkey" (raccoon) accounting for the bulk of the stomach contents.

Borderland prey examples are much more limited, but stomach contents have included horse, young and adult cattle, maggot-infested elk carrion, white-tailed deer, white-nosed coati, javelina, and desert tortoise. One jaguar was even found to have a stomach full of frogs (Table 1). Also of possible dietary interest is Warner Glenn's account of the jaguar brought to bay in the Peloncillo Mountains that smelled strongly of skunk. Other houndsmen have reported mountain lions also smelling strongly of skunk and these mustelids may be a more common prey item for big cats than previously realized.

Limited data and interviews suggest that the principal native prey of jaguars along the border are Coues white-tailed deer (Figure 20) and javelina, or collared peccary (Figure 21). The coati is also probably an important dietary item, and opossum and other medium mammals are probably also taken. It is an unfortunate fact, however, that as in so many

Figure 21. Javelina, or collared peccary. These small piglike animals are thought to be an important food source for borderland jaguars. Arizona Game and Fish Department photograph by Bob Miles.

other regions, borderland jaguars have taken to killing cattle, both because of convenience and out of necessity. With the depletion of such native game as white-tailed deer and javelina, the jaguar has little choice but to either become a cattle-killer or starve. Usually, but not always, the victims of these depredations are young animals—calves, yearlings, and small steers weighing less than 600 lb. And, cattle-killing jaguars have little reason to return to feeding on natural prey. Calves are favored by both jaguars and mountain lions, not only because cattle are so commonplace, but because they require less effort to locate and kill than wild game.

Hunting and Killing Methods

Jaguars are among the most nocturnal of all cats, being primarily active between dusk and dawn. The time from midmorning until midafternoon is invariably a time of rest, although individuals vary and weather conditions most likely play some role in the animals' activity patterns. Jaguars are also the most aquatic of all cats, readily taking to the water when opportunity and desire warrant. Foraging jaguars have been

Figure 22. Typical jaguar kill. Note the broken neck, lack of covering material, and that the head parts have been fed upon.

known to swim rivers more than a mile wide, and coastal swamps are favorite hunting grounds. Small drainages are frequent travelways, as tracks show that these cats favor walking on soft ground and sandy washes rather than hard rocks. An exception is areas where the leaf litter is so copious as to interfere with the animal's silent passage, in which case the animal may select the least noisy route.

Jaguars stalk cattle and other large animals and then attack from the rear or side. The usual mode of attack is to reach a paw over the prey's head, which is then pulled toward the cat until the victim falls to the ground. Often the prey's neck is broken in the process. More often than not, the jaguar will also sink its teeth into the back of the animal's neck just behind the ears. Death is usually relatively quick, especially if the cat is experienced. The carcass may then be dragged to some heavy cover, the jaguar sometimes displaying impressive strength and stamina in the process. Rarely, if ever, does the jaguar stash its prey in a tree, like a leopard, or cover its kill, like a mountain lion.

The jaguar typically eats the forward parts of large animals first, with the underside of the neck and chest usually being consumed immediately (Figure 22). Normally a jaguar does not return to a kill until after dark.

Any remaining bones are then crushed and rasped clean. According to hunters and ranchers familiar with depredation kills, jaguars digest their meals, which may be expansive, in about twelve hours and feed, on average, about once every three days.

Because both the mountain lion and protected jaguar are known stock killers in the American Southwest, some effort has been spent trying to separate the livestock-killing methods of these two cats. Jaguar kills typically have their first and second vertebrae dislocated, and prey animals often have bite marks on their face or nose. The claw marks, or "rakes," will likely be on the shoulders, ribs, and hind quarters, rather than just the flanks. Also, there will not usually be any marks indicating a suffocating grip on the throat. The first items consumed are typically the prey's head parts (e.g., ears, jaw, and nose), with the tongue appearing to be as much a favorite with the jaguar as the liver and heart is to the lion. Meat will also be taken at the first feeding from the neck, ribs, and both front shoulders. Very little bone may be eaten, and although the abdominal cavity may be opened on one side from ribs to flank, the internal organs are often ignored. By the end of the second feeding, little but a skeleton is left.

Mountain lions typically sink their claws in the prey's off-shoulder, then bite into the back of the neck. The size of the intended prey apparently determines the lion's killing behavior, a choke-hold being used more often on larger animals whose neck muscles are too thick to bite through. When a lion occasionally attempts to take down a yearling steer or other large animal by the nose, the would-be predator will usually suffer much abuse in the process, leaving copious amounts of hair on the ground. The neck area on mountain lion kills therefore usually shows bite marks, either from the cat biting the back of the neck or by biting the throat and suffocating the animal. The upper canine marks of a mountain lion will be from 1.75 in (4.4 cm) to 2.00 in (5.1 cm) apart, the lower canine marks between 1.25 in (3.2 cm) and 1.5 in (3.8 cm). Lion kills often also show a massive hemorrhage on the back of the neck and/or base of the skull. Of course, young animals are less adept at killing than more experienced ones, and as a result, blood stains may cover the ground where an animal wasn't immediately killed. The kill is then typically moved 30–75 ft (9.0–22.5 m) before the cat begins to feed. When feeding, the mountain lion usually enters the carcass just behind the rib cage, sometimes even breaking off a rib or two while doing so. The carcass is then eviscerated and the heart, liver, and lungs consumed; the paunch is not eaten, however, and is typically removed and buried. The larger leg muscles are the next parts eaten, the lion usually beginning on the inside of the hind leg. The remainder of the kill is then usually dragged to a burial site, commonly under a tree or in some other area where debris is readily available. Mountain lion kills in the borderlands area are almost always covered, even if the covering consists of only a few sticks and leaves—a characteristic that helps differentiate the kills of the two species more than any other. The lion may then bed down several hundred yards from the kill, from where the cat will make several return visits.

Wolf and dog kills invariably show damage to the prey's hind quarters, and animals fed on by bears are typically partially skinned. Coyotes do not often kill as cleanly as the big cats, and there is usually much blood and signs of a struggle in the vicinity of a kill. Bobcats tend to chew off the ears of their victims. All of this goes to show that reading sign and being able to differentiate the tracks of the various carnivores are important skills in determining which species of predators are present. The biggest problem in determining the predator of small animals—calf size and smaller—is that the prey is often entirely consumed at the first feeding. Even when parts of the carcass are left uneaten, carrion-feeding birds and mammals may consume or scatter whatever parts remain.

Some investigators have suggested that peccaries are more important prey items than deer to jaguars, the latter being a more staple food for lions. Certainly the ranges of peccaries and jaguars are largely sympatric. Our very limited data, however, neither support nor refute this contention. But, if the javelina is indeed the preferred prey of the jaguar, southern Arizona would be better habitat for jaguars now than in 1900, because these small, piglike animals have increased greatly both in numbers and distribution since 1950. Unfortunately, the jaguar was by then already gone from the United States for all practical purposes.

Breeding and Reproduction

Female jaguars reach sexual maturity when they are about two and a half years old. For physiological and social reasons, males take longer to mature in the wild, most becoming sexually active when they are between three and four years old. As the female comes into heat, or oestrus, she becomes more vocal and may range beyond her regular boundaries in search of a mate. Once a pair locate each other, they will often remain together as long as the female is in oestrus, the pair feeding but not hunting together.

The oestrus period lasts about nine days, an unbred female coming into heat again in about thirty days. Mating, as in all cats, is a hurried affair, more remarkable for its frequency than its duration. Copulation lasts less than thirty seconds, but may take place from ten to twenty times a day.

The gestation period, based on zoo animals, is about 100 days. Although no defined breeding season has been reported for jaguars in South America, most of the births of zoo animals in northern latitudes take place in the spring. This would support statements that the breeding season for Southwestern jaguars is in January and February and that the young are born in April or May, as was reported by an *Arizona Daily Star* article on jaguar cubs taken in the Chiricahuas. Spring birth dates are also indicated by the Lee brothers, who reported taking a female with a cub and another cub less than three months old, in central Sonora during the middle of the summer. Other sources in Sonora report jaguars giving birth during the winter, spring, and summer months, but especially between the end of the dry season in May and June and the beginning of the rainy season in late June and July. A. Starker Leopold (1959) stated that most of his Mexican informants told him that jaguars in Mexico had their young during the monsoon season between July and September—an opinion also relayed by J. H. Batty, after he collected a series of jaguars in the Marismas Nacionales in extreme southern Sinaloa. This would place the breeding season for these more southern jaguars in April and May. Only future studies will determine which, if any, of these generalities have any basis in fact. But it stands to reason that the peak period of birthing would be when prey is concentrated and the most vulnerable.

The usual litter size is two, although from one to four cubs may be born. In Sonora, most of the females that were accompanied by their young when killed had two cubs, although some of the females had only one. No one has yet reported more than two cubs in a litter. Some litter sizes may initially be higher, however, because kittens are not usually discovered until they are about three months old and exploring their new surroundings with their mother.

Den sites vary, but may consist of a natural cave, an abandoned mine, an overhang or copse of dense vegetation, or any other secluded site. The kittens at birth weigh between 30.0 and 30.5 oz (850 and 865 g) and measure just under 16 in (41 cm) in length. The eyes, which in very young cubs are blue, open from three to thirteen days after parturition (see Plate 5). The young will begin eating meat brought to them by their mother at ten to eleven weeks of age, with the mother keeping the den clean and nearly scentless by eating the kittens' feces. Although the cubs may continue to nurse until they are six months old, most young can be considered weaned when they are about twenty-two weeks of age. The young jaguars remain with their mother, learning to hunt, until they are one and a half to two years old and when their milk teeth have been replaced by permanent teeth. The young are then forced to either share part of the female's home range or find a territory for themselves. Although a young female may be allowed to share a portion of the mother's home range, young males are usually forced into unfamiliar territory to fend for themselves. These are the animals that most frequently show up in Arizona, Chihuahua, and other far-flung locales.

To compensate for their low reproductive potential, jaguars have a relatively long natural life span. Animals in captivity have been known to live between twenty and twenty-five years, and one individual was reported to have lived for thirty-two years. The potential for such a life expectancy in wild animals is, of course, less. The oldest jaguar that we recorded from the state of Sonora, its age estimated on the basis of tooth cementum annuli, was a female about thirteen years old. Assuming that she had her first litter at three years of age and that she has a litter of one to two cubs every two years thereafter, she would have produced from five to ten cubs during her lifetime. Few Southwestern jaguars probably live to be ten years old, however, and it is doubtful that the average female can raise more than three to six cubs to subadults. Fortunately, she has only to raise one female and one male to maturity for the population to maintain itself. Only such a population model can explain how a jaguar population as exploited as the one in central Sonora can sustain itself.

Population Characteristics of Southwestern Jaguars

The ratios of males to females killed in Arizona and Sonora is of some interest, especially when the factor of time is considered. All three of the animals killed or photographed in Arizona during the last quarter of the twentieth century were males, as were all the known animals taken in Chihuahua. This exclusivity of males likely indicates wandering or transient animals attempting to find a mate and/or set up a home range. A similar statement could also be made for jaguars killed in Arizona between 1925 and 1975, when eleven males are represented and only two females (Table 1). The situation is much different during the first quarter of the

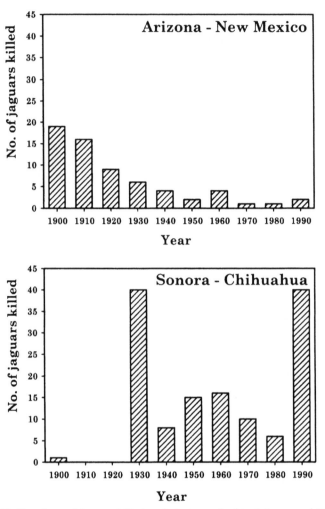

Figure 23. Numbers of jaguars killed and photographed in Arizona and New Mexico since 1900 by ten-year intervals (top) compared with the number killed in Sonora and Chihuahua (bottom). The bar graph from the American Southwest reflects a recorded history and shows a decline in jaguars over time. The northwestern Mexico data are based on both American records and remembered Mexican knowledge and show the continuing presence of jaguars in Sonora.

century, however, when six males, four females, and three young jaguars were reportedly taken in the American Southwest. Although young female jaguars may also become transients upon weaning, they are not as prone to wander as males and usually set up a home range within the area frequented by their mothers or in the nearest vacant niche providing suitable

Figure 24. Female jaguar killed in 1963 by Terry Penrod south of Big Lake, Arizona, at an elevation of 9100 ft (2730 m).

Figure 25. Jaguar shot by Laurence "Mickey" McGee in November 1965 while he was deer hunting in the Patagonia Mountains, Arizona.

prey. Considering the increasingly skewed sex ratio and pattern of decline in kills at ten-year intervals, one could argue that the jaguar population in the American Southwest, always thinly scattered, was overexploited during the twentieth century (Table 1, Figure 23). The last known female jaguar in Arizona was killed in 1963 (Figure 24), and a young male shot in 1965 (Figure 25) was the most recent possible subadult killed in the United States.

The situation is much different in Sonora: Of eighty-five sexed and aged jaguars killed during the twentieth century, forty-two were adult males, twenty-nine were adult females, and fourteen were cubs (Table 2). This figure of 50 percent males and 50 percent females and young is typical of an exploited but self-sustaining jaguar population in which most of the animals killed are actual or suspected stock killers. It will be interesting to see if this population continues to maintain these ratios under the heavy hunt pressure presently being experienced.

Home Ranges and Coexistence with Other Carnivores

The home ranges of jaguars are highly variable and depend on the topography, available prey, and the population density of the cats themselves. Little information is available on this subject outside of tropical America, where several studies of jaguar ecology have been conducted. The average home range size of radio-collared male jaguars in Venezuela was calculated to be between 19 and 30 sq mi (49 and 78 sq km). Females were not prone to range so widely, averaging less than 10–15 sq mi (26–39 sq km).

Four male jaguars in Belize's Cockscomb Basin had relatively small home ranges of 10.8–15.4 sq mi (28.0–39.9 sq km), while a female only used 4.2 sq mi (10.9 sq km). Female jaguars in the Chamela-Cuixmala Biosphere Reserve in Jalisco, Mexico, had home ranges of about 10 sq mi (26 sq km) during the dry season, but used approximately 25 sq mi (65 sq km) during the wet season, when game was less concentrated. The home ranges of borderland jaguars is presumably as large or larger, as is the distance young males will cover in their search for a territory. Using camera traps, we estimated the seasonal (winter-spring) range of a male jaguar in Sonora to be approximately 50 sq mi (130 sq km) before the animal was killed as a stock killer that same year.

The jaguar coexists throughout its range with the puma *(Puma concolor)*, known in the Southwest as the mountain lion. In South and Central America, pumas are said to differ from jaguars in their elevation preferences, prey selection, and habitat affinities. There is much overlap, however, and although jaguars in Central and South America have been reported to prefer wetter, lower sites and larger prey than pumas, such is not necessarily the case in Mexico and the American Southwest. On the Pacific coast of Mexico, at Chamela-Cuixmala Biosphere Reserve, jaguars and pumas have similar diets, habitats, and activity patterns. The principal separation mechanism appears to be spatial avoidance, the two species remaining at least 2.5 mi (4.0 km) apart. In the Southwest, jaguars never live in areas where mountain lions are absent, and the latter invariably outnumbers the former. In the Sahuaripa-Huasabas area of Sonora, however, camera traps record both species about equally. In the matter of prey selection, borderland jaguars may even be considered to be more catholic than lions, in that they also take a greater number of aquatic animals. Both cats readily take livestock, especially in areas where stocks of native game animals have been depleted—a jaguar sometimes paying the price for the actions of its colleague.

Other Behaviors

Almost all of the houndsmen who have successfully hunted both species state that the jaguar has more stamina than the mountain lion and is less prone to tree. When brought to bay, jaguars are as likely to hole up in a cave, minetunnel, rocky outcrop, or even a thicket as to climb a tree, although they will tree if a suitable one is available and other escape cover is lacking. The jaguar is also more likely to attack and kill pursuing dogs should one of the animals approach too closely. Indeed, several hunters reported coming upon jaguars and finding them to be remarkably bold and unwary. Perhaps they are just fearless, for several people have reported encountering jaguars and failing to interrupt the animal's activity; in several instances, a surprised jaguar acted as if the natural cover and his camouflaged coat rendered him invisible. Feeding jaguars also appeared unconcerned about human intruders, and in at least one instance, a jaguar challenged a hunter over a white-tailed deer the man had killed. Several hunters, none of whom were using dogs, reported coming upon a jaguar

Figure 26. Bonnie Swar-
brick posing with a
mounted ocelot trapped
in 1927 on the west side
of the Dragoon Moun-
tains, Cochise County,
Arizona.

less than 100 yards (90 m) away and shooting the animal as it was standing or crouched. Also, at least two jaguars were reportedly killed with
rocks!

Much has been said about the jaguar's swimming ability and propensity to take to the water. Yet, none of the borderland jaguars that we
recorded had taken to the water when pursued by houndsmen and their
dogs. The cats' inclination to swim may be a function of both opportunity
and climate, as both jaguars and mountain lions are known to take to the
water and swim long distances on occasion. As long as temperatures are
not too cold, mountain lions readily swim across reservoirs, and the tendency for jaguars to prefer water more than their mountain lion cousins
may be an overstatement. Nonetheless, an anecdote relayed by Sewell
Goodwin is of some interest in that he is the only houndsman in Arizona
whose dogs have trailed a jaguar, an ocelot, and mountain lions. He noted

that, while trailing a jaguar down Ciénega Creek after a summer shower, the jaguar, unlike most lions, never broke its stride to avoid stepping in water. Indeed, the jaguar left tracks in the bottom of a 10 ft wide pool.

Status of Other Borderland Cats

During the courses of our investigations, we had the opportunity to note the presence of mountain lions, bobcats, and ocelots as well as jaguars. Mountain lions are present everywhere jaguars are in the borderlands. Lions generally outnumber their spotted cousins, however, and except for transient males, both species are generally absent from the arid deserts of western Arizona and Sonora. Whether jaguars formerly occupied some of the mountain ranges west of Mexican Highway 15, as lions presently do, is unknown, but at least one reliable observer reported finding a dead jaguar on the beach near Libertad, Sonora (Table 2). Nonetheless, only a handful of jaguars have been reportedly killed west of the highway, where we have found both lion tracks and kills.

Bobcats *(Lynx rufus)* range throughout the mountains and broken country of the Southwest. Known in Sonora as *gato pochi,* or "bob-tailed cat," these felids appear to be absent or only present in low numbers in the arid plains of the Gran Desierto in extreme southwestern Arizona and northwestern Sonora and possibly the more arid reaches of the Gulf Coast.

Since 1900 only two ocelots *(Leopardus pardalis)* have been reportedly killed in Arizona (Figure 26), but hunters in Sonora who had killed jaguars had often also taken ocelots, or *gato galavis* (Figure 27). During our investigations, we documented thirty-nine ocelots taken in Sonora (Table 9). More than 60 percent of these cats were killed in Sinaloan thornscrub with another 20 percent (including the one well-documented Arizona specimen) taken in Madrean evergreen woodland. Although only five animals are known from Sinaloan tropical deciduous forest, this lower number reflects the fact that most of our work has been to the north of this biotic community. We therefore conclude that the primary biotic affinity of this animal in Sonora is with tropical thornscrub and tropical deciduous forest, with the ocelot occasionally ranging upward into Madrean evergreen woodland. Both tropical deciduous forest and thornscrub are generally lacking in Arizona, and this cat should not be considered a resident animal in the American Southwest.

Figure 27. Ocelot taken near San Javier, Sonora, in 1998. There is no question that this cat is an ocelot, and the photo is consistent with the politically incorrect use of dead cats in posing them with young girls and not-so young women.

We know of no specimens of jaguarundis *(Herpailurus yagouaroundi)* from either Arizona or Sonora. The jaguarundi cubs reportedly caught in Sonora in the early 1960s by the Arizona Game and Fish Department were actually captured in the Mexican state of Nayarit. We also believe that the other jaguarundi sightings reported for Arizona and Sonora by the Arizona Game and Fish Department are in error. During this study, we visited seventy-two *municipios* in Sonora and conducted hundreds of interviews with ranchers, vaqueros, hunters, trappers, livestock officials, and other rural residents. Most of these people were aware of jaguars, mountain lions, ocelots, and bobcats, and showed us skulls and hides of all of these cats. Yet, no one claimed to have seen a jaguarundi, nor did anyone recognize a picture of one of these diurnal cats when one was shown to them. We have therefore concluded that this species is confined to extreme southern Sonora, if it occurs anywhere in the region.

Table 9. Ocelots killed or photographed in Arizona and Sonora, 1887–2000.

Date	Collector/Reporter	Sex	Location/Municipo	Biotic Community[1]
12/24/2000	Camera trap photograph.	M	Rancho Zetasora, Sahuaripa	Madrean evergreen woodland
2000	*Vaquero*. Skin seen; photographs.	M	Rancho Tapila, Agua Prieta	Madrean evergreen woodland
2000	*Vaquero*. Skin seen; photographs.	M	Sierra Los Chinos, Sahuaripa	Madrean evergreen woodland
1999	*Vaquero*. Skin seen. Circumstances unknown.	M	Basopa, Sahuaripa	Sinaloan thornscrub
1999	Rancher. Photograph.	M	Rancho La Placita, Sahuaripa	Sinaloan thornscrub
1999	Rancher. Skin seen.	M	Rancho Los Taraices, Aconchi	Madrean evergreen woodland
1999	Rancher. Skin seen.	M	Sierra de Alamos, Alamos	Sinaloan deciduous forest
1999	Rancher. Skin seen.	F	Rosario de Tezopaco	Sinaloan thornscrub
1999	Rancher. Skin seen.	immature M	10 km W Tezapaco, Rosario	Sinaloan thornscrub
1997	Houndsman. Photograph.	M	Sierra de los Chinos, Sahuaripa	Sinaloan thornscrub
1995	Houndsman.	F	San Javier	Sinaloan thornscrub
1995	Houndsman. Photograph.	M	San Javier	Sinaloan thornscrub
1995	Rancher. Skin seen.	F	Río Moctezuma, Moctezuma	riparian within Sinaloan thornscrub
1995	Rancher. Skin seen.	M	Río Moctezuma, Moctezuma	riparian within Sinaloan thornscrub
1994	*Fide* Dr. Juan Pablo Gallo.	M	Granados/Sahuaripa	Sinaloan thornscrub
1994	Rancher.	M	Rancho San Vicente, Quiriego	Sinaloan thornscrub
1993	Rancher.	M	Arroyo de la Junta, Ures	Sinaloan thornscrub
before 1992	*Fide* Peter Warren of The Nature Conservancy.	?	E of Soyopa, Soyopa	Sinaloan thornscrub
before 1992	*Fide* Peter Warren. Animal taken to Centro Ecologico de Sonora in Hermosillo.	F?	Tonichi	Sinaloan thornscrub
1991	Houndsman.	?	Bacanora	Sinaloan thornscrub
before 1990	Rancher.	M	Rancho de los Nogales, Opodepe	Sinaloan thornscrub
1989	*Fide* Pete Manes. Road kill. Photograph.	F	Hwy 9, Rosario	Sinaloan deciduous forest
1988–1989	*Fide* Sr. Arturo Ortega.	?	Rancho La Montosa	Sinaloan thornscrub
1974	Bill Robinson et al. (houndsmen). Length 49 in.	?	Near Casitas, Nogales	Madrean evergreen woodland
1970	Kelly Neal saw trapped animal.	?	Rancho El Valle, Arizpe	Madrean evergreen woodland
1966	Sewell Goodwin, L. Elias, et al. (houndsmen). Photograph.	M	Sierra Piñitos E of Casitas, Nogales	Madrean evergreen woodland
1964	Sewell Goodwin and Ted Ferguson (houndsmen). Photograph.	M	Pat Scott Peak, Huachuca Mts., Arizona	Madrean evergreen woodland
?	Rancher.	?	San Pedro de la Cueva	Madrean evergreen woodland/Sinaloan thornscrub
?	Rancher. Skin seen in Hermosillo.	?	Nacori Chico, Baviacora	Sinaloan thornscrub

Table 9. Ocelots killed or photographed in Arizona and Sonora, 1887–2000, continued.

Date	Collector/Reporter	Sex	Location/Municipo	Biotic Community
?	Hunter. Skin seen in Hermosillo.	?	?	?
?	Hunter. Skin seen in Hermosillo.	?	N of Ures	Sinaloan thornscrub
?	Hunter. Skin seen in Hermosillo.	?	Suaqui Grande	Sinaloan thornscrub
1935	Dale Lee et al. McCurdy 1979.	?	Junction of Rios Aros and Bavispe, Sahuaripa	Sinaloan thornscrub
before 1938	W. H. Burt 1938.	?	Guirocoba, S of Alamos	Sinaloan thornscrub
1931–1932	Unknown Predator and Rodent Control agent.	?	southern Arizona	?
1927	Trapped by M. Stewart. Mounted and photographed by L. O. Woolery. Reported in *Tombstone Epitaph*.	?	West side of Dragoon Mts., Cochise Co., Arizona	semidesert grass-land/Madrean evergreen woodland
2/1900	Mr. McLean. Reported in *Field and Stream* 1900, 6(2):165.	? small	Near Guadalupe on Río Aros, 28°30'N, 108°40'W	Sinaloan thornscrub
1898	Collected by E. A. Goldman for U.S. National Museum.	3 M + 1 F	Near Camoa, Alamos	Sinaloan deciduous forest
1887	E. A. Mearns. Sent to American Museum of Natural History.	?	Arizona	?

1. Biotic communities from Brown (1994).

2

Jaguars and People

Tiger's skin is prized above all because of its beauty: therefore, he who has slain a tiger is proud and happy.

Ignaz Pfefferkorn (1989)

Men and jaguars have been interacting in the Western Hemisphere for at least 11,000 years but, because the jaguar is the top predator throughout its range, this animal has always enjoyed a special status among those it came in contact with. Like the puma, crocodile, and other large powerful animals, the jaguar has always been regarded as a metaphor for power, strength, and predatory behavior—so much so that the animal frequently played a prominent role in religion, mythology, art, and iconography. Indeed, motifs of large felids are one of several items separating Middle American cultures from the ursine-orientated peoples inhabiting more northern regions. This is certainly true in the American Southwest, where long-tailed cats can be seen in rock art, on pottery designs, in kiva murals, and even as sculptured figures.

The name "jaguar" continues to invoke much awe and reverence among the native peoples of Amazonia. Even today, shamans in South America wear headdresses of upturned jaguar claws and necklaces of jaguar teeth and carry bags made of jaguar hide, which contain their herbs, stones, and magical snuffs. Narcotic powders are kept in tubular jaguar bones, and a shaman may paint black spots on his face in imitation of a jaguar. The most honored status of the jaguar, however, was achieved during the reigns of the great Native American civilizations that formerly occupied Mesoamerica.

The Jaguar in Prehistoric Cultures

Sometime prior to 1500 B.C., a cult developed among the prehistoric peoples inhabiting the tropical rain forests and swamps along the Gulf of Mexico in what is now southern Veracruz, Tabasco, and Campeche. These people, destined to create the first complex civilization in North America, traded in jaguar skins and adopted this animal as their principal totem. This civilization, which we now call the Olmec culture, elevated the jaguar to the same status as the deity providing rain and used jaguar masks and capes to ornament the costumes of warriors, nobles, and priests. The jaguar is believed to have symbolized a cave god who controlled the land (and earthquakes), while a feathered serpent was the analogous deity for water. Commonly taking its animal form in his nightly peregrinations, this jaguar deity, when joined by his serpent counterpart, formed a supernatural were-jaguar that controlled life itself. Later, as the culture developed, the Olmecs used characters symbolizing jaguar muzzles, claws, rosettes, and other body parts as a stylistic form of writing to describe the mysteries of fecundity, birth, and other phenomena.

Olmec jaguar representations tended to be symbolic, rather than representative, and can be seen as cave paintings, carved jade effigies, terra cotta figures, and stone statues, some of which are thought to depict jaguar-people resulting from a woman copulating with a jaguar or were-jaguar. These jaguar-people typically possess Mongoloid features, and the Olmecs may have considered such human children to have been the manifestation of were-jaguars. For whatever reason, Mongoloid-like figures and colossal sculptured heads (including a basalt monolith in the form of a jaguar's head) are trademarks of Olmec culture. A number of these gigantic statues, as well as a strange floor mosaic of a stylized jaguar, have been taken to La Venta Park near Villahermosa, Tabasco, where they can be seen today. It is also significant that the largest Olmec structure yet discovered is the ceremonial House of the Jaguar, which is believed to have been built for the jaguar god and his priests.

Over time, Olmec cultural features such as ball courts, the feathered serpent motif, and jaguar worship expanded southward to Colombia; westward to Guerrero, Mexico; and possibly even as far north as the American Southwest. Based on skeletal material found in archeological sites, it is thought that certain Olmec rites involved sacrificing jaguars along with pumas, turkeys, and humans. As Olmec culture expanded, however, it also declined; by 400 B.C. it was being eclipsed by such great city and religious

Figure 28. Olmec terra cotta jaguar figure at Cicom Museum in Villahermosa, Tabasco. Note the collar, which indicates a captive animal.

centers as El Tajín in Veracruz, Xochicalco and Teotihuacán on the Mexican Plateau, Monte Albán in Oaxaca, and the Mayan cities of the Guatemalan highlands. It was also during this period that some of the finest jaguar artifacts were produced. In addition to full-bodied stone replicas and snarling heads, these artifacts included intricately decorated funeral sensors, exquisite jade pendants, and wheeled pull-toys. The Cicom Museum of Olmec culture in Villahermosa, Tabasco, displays some excellent examples of jaguarlike masks and figurines, depicting both jaguar-people and the jaguars themselves (Figure 28).

The cultures that supplanted the Olmecs and built the great religious centers at Teotihuacán, Monte Albán, and other Middle American sites between 700 B.C. and 750 A.D. while retaining such Olmec influences as ball courts and altars for human sacrifice, were not always located in prime jaguar habitat. Possibly for this reason, jaguars were raised in captivity, as indicated by recent excavations under the Temple of the Moon in Teotihuacán, which have revealed cages containing the remains of both jaguars

Figure 29. Zapotec jaguar
(or possibly puma) from
Monte Albán, Oaxaca, Mexico.
Photograph taken in the
National Museum of
Anthropology, Mexico City.

and their droppings. Many of the so-called jaguar depictions at Teotihuacán and Monte Alban are also highly stylized, and some of the carica-
tures may actually represent pumas or various combinations of these two
felids. Almost all of the jaguarlike animals that appear in murals, on pottery vessels, as clay figurines, and as masks are composites of jaguars and
other animals or they resemble humans in jaguar costumes. Even those
animals that look the most like jaguars usually possess birdlike eyes or
feathers and typically have bodies laced with netting or spotted with flow-
ers or seashells rather than rosettes.

With the general chaos that accompanied the decline of Teotihuacán
and the other great city-states, other cultures such as the Mixtecs, Za-
potecs, and Toltecs took up the jaguar motif. In the process, however, the
jaguar appears to have become less of a deity and more of a religious
metaphor. At least the images of the animal become less convoluted (Figure 29). The Zapotec and Mixtec cultures replaced their original rain god,
Cocijo, with a man-eating jaguar that was depicted in both human and
felid form. One Zapotec site, Dainzú in Oaxaca, contains a tomb entrance

in the form of a jaguar carved in three pieces: the two vertical legs supporting a lintel taking the form of a rather realistic head and shoulders.

Living in southern Mexico, Guatemala, and Honduras, it was only natural that the Mayan culture shared the Olmec's fascination with jaguars. Known in their various languages as *baalam* or *bolum*, the jaguar was synonymous with fierceness, strength, and bravery; the animal and its parts assumed the role of power symbols. A jaguar mat was the seat of Mayan authority, and "spreading the jaguar skin" was the term used for going to war. Jaguar costumes (including the black phase) were worn by persons of authority and were depicted on polychrome jars, on stelae and other statuary, in Mayan codices, and in various other media. Such costumes required a steady supply of skins, and jaguar pelts were highly valued as trade items (Figure 30). Both jaguars and pumas were ritually sacrificed, and to combat any scarcity, animals were specifically raised for this purpose. Jaguar bones and droppings have been found in a burial tomb in Palenque, Chiapas, just as they were at Teotihuacán.

Because it was classified as a powerful animal along with the puma and the rattlesnake, the jaguar also had a prominent role in Mayan mythology. The jaguar was closely associated with the sun god, Kinich Ahau, who would transform himself into a jaguar during his nightly journey through the underworld. Also, the mythical Mayan twins, Hunahpú and Xbalanque, who play a crucial role in the Mayan creation myth, are often marked like jaguars in art and writing. Hunahpú has large black spots on his cheeks and body, whereas Xbalanque displays jaguar skin patches around his mouth and on his torso and limbs.

The militaristic Toltec culture that occupied Teotihuacán in 650 A.D. and eventually dominated central and southern Mexico brought jaguar and puma iconography to a new level of symbolism depicting war and power. After sacking Teotihuacán, the Toltecs not only adopted the feathered serpent, Quetzalcoatl, as their chief deity, they also restructured the old were-jaguar and jaguar metaphors into symbols for warfare. Now regarded more as a military logo than a religious motif, jaguar art became increasingly realistic—an iconography that emphasized current fantasy rather than any celestial message (Figure 31). Not only did the Toltecs depict jaguars and serpents eating the hearts of their enemies and prisoners, the pairing of jaguars and eagles as the twin symbols of warfare became a popular theme at the Toltec capitol of Tula (Tollan).

As the Toltecs spread throughout Middle America, so did their concepts and symbolism. By around 500 A.D. both jaguars and pumas were

Figure 30. Maya
codex showing the
presentation of a
jaguar pelt. Photo-
graph taken in the
National Museum
of Anthropology,
Mexico City.

favorite artistic and ceremonial motifs in the Guatemalan Highlands, the
Yucatán Peninsula, southern and southwestern Mexico, and in the Valley
of Mexico, even though the last site was not typical jaguar habitat. It is uncertain how far south and north the Toltec culture and its fascination with
jaguars spread, but there is good evidence that its influences, at least, extended as far south as northwestern Costa Rica and as far north as the
American Southwest. Wherever the Toltecs went, jaguar symbolism prolif-
erated. A temple atop the famous pyramid known as El Castillo at
Chichén-Itzá, a postclassic Mayan religious center showing many Toltec
influences, contain a jaguar throne carved out of a great block of lime-

Figure 31. Toltec portrait of a jaguar. Photograph taken in the National Museum of Anthropology, Mexico City.

stone. Painted in brilliant cinnabar, the statue is studded in seventy-three jade spots. The eyes, too, are jade, and the white canine teeth are made of flint (Figure 32). At the same site there is also a Temple of the Jaguars, so named because it contains a Toltec frieze depicting a procession of jaguars as well as a free-standing altar in the form of a jaguar. As if this were not enough feline symbolism, a free-standing sculpture of a double-headed felid dominates a position across from the nearby Palace of the Governors.

The Aztecs, the Nahuatl-speaking warrior-merchants who vanquished the Toltecs and who were in turn conquered by the Spaniards in 1519, raised jaguar iconography to its highest level. Ocelotl, as the jaguar was

Figure 32. Postclassic Mayan (Toltec) jaguar sculpture: the cinnabar jaguar of Chichén-Itzá. Museum figure drawn by Randy Babb.

called, was regarded by the Aztecs as the bravest and fiercest of animals, whose cautious, wise, and proud disposition made it the ruler of the animal world. Ocelotl, therefore, became a metaphor for warriors, dignitaries, and rulers—the Aztec elite. Aztec emperors adorned themselves in jaguar capes, breechclouts, and sandals; wore insignias of jaguar skin into battle; and retained the exclusive use of jaguar hide thrones, mats, and cushions as symbols of authority. The Aztec's nocturnal deity, Tezcatlipoca, was considered the jaguar's alter ego and the patron of sorcerers, who employed jaguar claws, jaguar pelts, and jaguar hearts in their rituals.

Two elite military orders, the Eagle Knights and the Jaguar Knights, had the duty of guarding the emperor and the Aztec capitol of Tenochtitlan (today's Mexico City). Aztec codices show these warriors wearing jaguar and eagle costumes, both adorned with elaborate feathered headdresses, into battle (Figure 33). Tenochtitlan's chief edifice, the Templo Mayor, also contained a huge feline sculpture with a hollowed-out back to receive sacrificial human hearts (Figure 34). Excavations at this site, which are still incomplete, revealed not only jaguar and puma burial offerings,

Figure 33. The Aztec Codex Mendoza showing the apparel of Jaguar Warrior. Codex figures redrawn by Randy Babb.

Figure 34 (below). Aztec jaguar sculpture from Tenochtitlán. Photograph taken in the National Museum of Anthropology, Mexico City.

Figure 35. Huichol jaguar mask. Photograph taken in the National Museum of Anthropology, Mexico City.

but also facilities for raising these cats. At least one such animal, a puma, was interned in its entirety with an alabaster ball in its mouth. Another ceremonial site, Malinalco, was hewed out of a limestone hillside and contains stone jaguars cut from the same rock, the animals crouching on each side of a stairway that leads into a room containing alternating sculptures of eagles and jaguars. Archeologists believe that such "warrior houses" were meeting halls for the two orders and that these sites came under the protection of a special god.

In Aztec religious mythology, the great god Tezcatlipoca was usually depicted as a jaguar. According to myths, he was knocked from the sky by Quetzalcoatl, the feathered serpent, fell into the sea, and was changed into a Great Jaguar. In the Aztec creation myth, there were four previous worlds, or suns, each named and identified with a particular deity and race of people. Each world was also linked to one of the elements—earth, wind, fire, and water, which would eventually destroy that particular world. The earth world, for example, was named Nahui Ocelotl (Four Jaguar) and was destroyed by jaguars—creatures closely associated with the land.

The Aztecs also had a myth about Teotihuacán, which was abandoned by the time they arrived. The Aztec story was that the gods had gathered there in darkness after the destruction of the fourth sun and had elected two of their number, the haughty Tecuciztecatl and the humble Nanahuatzin, to sacrifice themselves in a great fire so that a new world would return. After his courage failed him once and seeing the heroic Nanahuatzin sacrifice himself, Tecuciztecatl leaped into the flames. Seeing the heroism of the gods, the eagle and jaguar did likewise. This act is evidenced by the scorched appearance of the eagle's feathers and the black smudges on the jaguar's pelt. Tecuciztecatl and Nanahuatzin then became the gods of the sun and the moon, respectively, while the eagle and jaguar went on to become the two great Aztec military orders.

With the Spanish Conquest, the great religious and symbolic nature of the jaguar came to an end. Although such far-flung cultures as the Tarascan, Huichol, and Huasteca retained the use of jaguar imagery (Figure 35), the animal's role as a deity and herald had passed its apogee.

Jaguars and the Prehistoric Indians of the Southwest

Long-tailed cats are one of the most common depictions in Southwestern rock art, the vast majority of which is prehistoric in origin. Other catlike figures are depicted in pictographs, on pottery, and as stone effigies. Depending on their location, these "lions," a few of which appear to be spotted, are thought to be the work of such prehistoric cultures as the Hohokam, Mimbres, Casa Grande, and Anasazi—civilizations known to have ball courts and to have been influenced by Mesoamerican concepts. Although it has been commonly assumed that these cats were all mountain lions, many native Southwestern peoples speak a Uto-Aztecan-derived language, and at least some of their depictions, which also include horned serpents, macaws, and other Mexican motifs, may have been northern manifestations of jaguar symbolism or even jaguar worship. The bodies of some catlike petroglyphs, for example, contain netted designs and other markings reminiscent of jaguar portrayals in Middle America (Figure 36).

Probably the most realistic animal images from the prehistoric Southwest are on Mimbres pottery. The Mimbres culture occupied southwestern

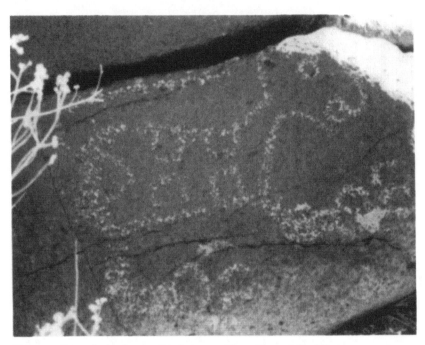

Figure 36. Petroglyph of a possible jaguar at Three Rivers, New Mexico.
Photograph by Thomas Hulen.

New Mexico and southeastern Arizona between 1000 and 1250 A.D. and
was contemporary with the nearby Casa Grande culture to the south, the
Anasazi culture to the north, and the Toltec culture of the Mexican
Plateau. The rich artistic legacy of the Mimbres includes the depiction of a
number of easily recognized animals, such as pronghorn antelope,
bighorn sheep, macaw, Montezuma quail, Gambel's quail, and Gila chub.
A number of Mexican motifs have also been recovered from Mimbres
archeological sites, including copper bells, ball courts, portrayals of
horned serpents, and a bowl showing a decapitation scene that may represent a human sacrifice. Felids are well represented among the pottery designs, and some of these cats could be interpreted as being jaguars or
jaguar-lion combinations, in that their bodies are filled in with various ab-
stract designs and the tails are distinctly striped.

Murals in prehistoric Pueblo kivas also contain representations of animals that might be jaguars. One such site, Awatovi in Jeddito Valley, Arizona, near the Hopi villages on Antelope Mesa, is especially interesting.
This site was excavated in 1939, and the murals were dated (through the
use of tree rings) to have been produced between 1411 and 1430 A.D.

Figure 37. Mural depicting a jaguar in a kiva at Broken Pottery Ruin, New Mexico. Used with permission of Dr. Frank Hibben.

Some of these murals show catlike figures, macaws, and what appears to be an imperial woodpecker. One of the cats is ventrally spotted, black on blue gray, dorsally scalloped, and might have been intended to be a composite of a mountain lion and a jaguar. The posterior half of another cat is white with black spots, and both animals have barred tails similar to a jaguar's.

Between 1958 and 1961 Frank Hibben excavated some intriguing murals, which were meticulously copied by Nancy Atkins and Tom Bahti. The murals were found in seventeen kivas at Pottery Mound in northern New Mexico, near the Rio Puerco. This site was dated at between 1300 and 1475 A.D. and contains a number of Mexican (i.e., Toltec and Aztec) motifs. These include paintings of scarlet macaws, six plumed serpents (Quetzalcoatl), an imperial woodpecker and its feathers, and a spectacular black-on-orange jaguar accompanied by an eagle and a flayed-faced Xipes, god of renewal (Figure 37). Two mountain lions in the same fresco also have a distinctive Mexican flavor, and there is a strangulation scene that might depict a human sacrifice. The murals are thought to be religious in nature rather than artistic. Another even-finer jaguar painting was said to be badly damaged and unable to be reproduced. The artist at Broken Pottery Ruin had almost certainly seen a jaguar or at least the hide of one.

Another prehistoric cat reproduction in the Southwest's Pueblo region is the Shrine of the Stone Lions near the ruins of Yapashenye on Portrero de las Vacas in what is now Bandelier National Monument in New Mex-

Figure 38. Shrine of the Stone Lions in Bandelier National Monument, New Mexico. The nearer, heftier cat's tail length is 41 percent of the statue's total length, whereas the rear figure's tail is 50 percent the total length.

ico's Jemez Mountains. These figures, considered to be the foremost hunting shrine in the Southwest, are thought to date to the fourteenth century. Consisting of two cats carved in relief out of the native tufa, the animals are crouched side by side, tails extended, and facing east (Figure 38). Now weather worn but still impressive, these life-sized effigies are enclosed within a crude pentagon of rocks. Could one of these paired cats have been intended to represent a jaguar? The tail of the more mottled cat is approximately 41 percent of the statue's head and body length, whereas the tail of the other cat is almost exactly 50 percent of the head and body length. These respective dimensions are very close to those of a jaguar and a mountain lion. The surrounding ancient pueblos are rife with ball courts and other Mexican-derived concepts. Why not jaguar iconography?

The Jaguar in Contemporary Southwestern Native Cultures

As with other contemporary native peoples, the Cahita-speaking Yaqui and Mayo Indians revere the jaguar, or *yoco,* more as an esteemed game animal than for any supposed supernatural powers. Ethnologist Edward Spicer (1985) did not even include the jaguar in his list of animals important to the Yaquis, and none of the more than sixty Yaqui stories related by R. H. Giddings (1959) features a jaguar. Similarly, no mention of

Figure 39. Jaguar-hide chaps worn by an Indian vaquero near San Bernardo, Sonora, circa 1908. Photograph 62002, courtesy of the Arizona Historical Society, Tucson.

jaguars was found in any of the ethnological works on the Mayo people of Sonora. Jaguars nonetheless show up in several Cahita place names, such as Yocobampo ("jaguar in water") and Yocojigua ("food of the jaguar"; see also Table 7).

H. Scott Gentry (1963), who studied the Guarijio in the 1930s when they were still primarily a hunting-and-gathering people living in the remote *barrancas* of southern Sonora and Chihuahua, made no reference to any religious or mythological roles played by jaguars. And, although the Tarahumara of the Sierra Madre have always been well acquainted with jaguars, neither Karl Lumholtz nor his ethnologist successors, Bennett and Zingg (1935), recorded these peoples attributing any religious significance to these animals. Nor does J. A. Mason (1952) make any mention of jaguars in his book on Tepehuán religion and mythology. Indeed, these ethnographers, while reporting that they often saw jaguar skins among the Tarahumara, suggested that their principal value was to sell to the Mexicans "as decorations for their riding gear, etc." (Figure 39). This pragmatic view is also held by the Tepehuán people to the south of the Tarahumara.

When a *tigre*, which does much damage upon wandering pigs and goats, is reported as roaming a specific area, the Tepehuán attempt to locate the animal and hold it at bay with dogs until assistance can be obtained from someone who has a firearm. Should the jaguar be secured, its hide may be sold or used as a highly valued sleeping mat.

As for the Seri, a contemporary hunting-and-gathering people, WJ McGee (1895–1896) was told that the big game animals in their country included, along with the mountain sheep and mule deer, "the ubiquitous coyote, a puma, a jaguar of much local repute which roams the higher rocky sites, and a peccary." Twenty-five years later, the Seris told Charles Sheldon (1993) that "jaguars were rare on Tiburón Island, cougars not common; along with coyotes, jack rabbits and mule deer, these animals swimming back and forth from the mainland." The Seris related that the jaguar eats out the throat and heart of his kills and takes little more, while the mountain lion eats it all. The Seris also told Sheldon that jaguars were present on Isla Angel de la Guardia, an erroneous assumption on the part of the Indians, who had no firsthand knowledge of this island.

Opatas and Eudives

Father Juan Nentvig (1980), an early chronicler of Indian life in northern Sonora in the second half of the eighteenth century, described the jaguar's depredations on the Indian's herds: "The tiger, *tutzi* in Opata, is found throughout the province, is fiercer and does more harm to beasts of burden and cattle than does the lion, but does not attack man unless cornered."

Father Nentvig went on to state why the good grazing lands around Huasabas Mission along the Río Bavispe in east-central Sonora were no longer used for raising horses and cattle: "It is depopulated at present because of the Apache menace. Even on the river meadows and nearby hills, somewhat distant from the mission, the good grazing fields for all kinds of stock are of little or no use since the horse-herd is corralled every night— for what stays out runs the risk of not being there in the morning. Also cattle raising is uncertain because of the many tigers, lions and wolves that the rugged country shelters."

Pimas and Papagos

Another early Jesuit missionary, Ignaz Pfefferkorn (in Treutlein 1949), described the "Sonorans" (possibly the Sobaipuris) using quivers made of jaguar hide and gave reasons why the pelts of these animals were so valued:

> War bonnets are worn in engagements to give the wearers a horrible appearance and to frighten the enemy. These bonnets are made of the heads of the most terrible wild animals, which have been skinned with the greatest care and caution to prevent damage. The skins are stuffed, dried, and dressed so ingeniously that the face of the animal completely retains its high-spirited natural appearance. The head is the front part of the bonnet and covers the Indian's forehead, representing with great naturalness the terrible appearance of a tiger, a bear, or some other animal with pointed ears, gaping jaws, and terrible teeth. The back part of the bonnet covering the warrior's head to his ears is made of other parts of the animal's skin, decorated all around with many-colored feathers hanging from it. Finally, the bonnet is topped with a luxuriant feather plume.

Charles DiPeso (1953), who has conducted extensive studies on the Sobaipuri of southeastern Arizona, remarked that the parrots and macaws that supplied the feathers for these war bonnets were raised at San Xavier del Bac and other Pima *rancherias*. Also tantalizing is F. W. Hodge's (1910) reference to the Sobaipuri's habit of painting spots on their bodies. But, despite such obvious parallels with Aztec jaguar warriors, none of the eighteenth-century chroniclers mentions *tigres* as having any magical or religious significance to these tribes.

More recently, ethnologist C. W. Pennington (1980) reported that the Pima Bajo of Sonora considered the jaguar to be quite common at the higher elevations east and west of Onavas. These animals were hunted with dogs and the meat occasionally eaten. The skins were sold locally, kept as ornaments about the house, and used for decorative purposes, just as they are today.

Jaguars were also well known among the Papagos and other Pima-speaking Indians in Arizona, who referred to these cats as *oosha*, the spotted one (Rea 1998). Like the Sobaipuri and Pima Bajo, these Pima speakers considered the jaguar a game animal. It was sometimes eaten and the hide was valued for making quivers, headdresses, and other decorative objects. Amadeo Rea's Pima informants told him that, being a familiar animal to their southern ancestors, *oosha* was not considered a source of "sickness" and need not be avoided—the jaguar was not spiritually dangerous if not handled according to ritual. The animal was nonetheless regarded as a powerful hunter who could transfer hunting prowess through dreams. In one Pima myth related by Frances Densmore (1929), Elder Brother (the chief Pima deity) has a sister who is wooed by the four best hunters: Jaguar, Mountain Lion, Golden Eagle, and Peregrine Falcon. But she confounds everybody, including her brother, by marrying Gopher.

Not surprisingly, the Yavapai Indians of central Arizona had only an imperfect knowledge of jaguars and do not appear to have invoked any particular ritualism for this rare animal. E. W. Gifford's (1932) Yavapai informants told him of a "tiger," or *imita*, that was larger than a wildcat, orange-buff in color, and not the same animal as the mountain lion *(numita)*. Ethnologists do not record the Havasupai or Hualapai peoples as having any special relationships with jaguars, nor does Leslie Spier (1970) mention jaguars or jaguar lore among the Yuman tribes living along the lower Colorado River.

Neither G. Goodwin (1942) nor M. E. Opler (1965) record the jaguar as having any special significance among the Apaches other than that the animal's skins were valued for making arrow quivers and that these big cats were sometimes eaten. The Apaches were aware of jaguars, however, and according to F. Uplegger (1990) had a name for these "tigers": *nduithlikizhzhi*. Keith Basso (1971) also reported Apaches invoking "jaguar power" when pouncing on an opponent, much like a jaguar or a mountain lion would.

Of special interest is the possible role of jaguars in the religion and mythology of today's Pueblo Indians. L. A. White (1943) described a Rohona in the Kersan language, which is spoken in some of the pueblos in northwestern New Mexico and northwestern Arizona (e.g., Laguna, Acoma, and Hopi). Rohona was described by White's various informants as a weasel, a female mountain lion, or, as at Acoma and Santa Ana, a large spotted cat, that is, a jaguar. White's colleagues also told him that Rohona aided hunters in their quests for big game and was a sort of patron saint of big game hunters. As such, Rohona was often associated with the mountain lion in songs and ceremonies and is so shown on some kiva murals. That jaguars were the subject of particular reverence is also attested to by reports of some Hopis taking great care in dressing and preserving the skin of an "old" male jaguar that they had tracked down and killed in the snow 4 mi (6.4 km) south of the Grand Canyon during the winter of

Figure 40. Hide of a jaguar killed by Hopi Indians during the winter of 1907–1908 near the Grand Canyon in Arizona. Photograph from Billingsley (1971).

1907–1908 (Figure 40). One wonders if this reverence for jaguars might not have had its origins in the distant past, when these pueblo-dwelling peoples were subjected to strong Mexican influences.

Anglo-Americans and Borderland Jaguars

James Ohio Pattie (1905) was the first Anglo-American to report seeing a jaguar in what is today the Southwest. Pattie reported that his party killed an "animal not unlike the African leopard" during the winter of 1827–1828, while camped just upstream from the delta of the lower Colorado River, near the present boundary between Sonora and Baja California Norte. If this animal was indeed a jaguar, it was killed some 350 mi (560 km) northwest of what can be considered present-day jaguar habitat.

The next American to report seeing a Southwestern jaguar was J. Wayne, an assistant surveyor on Emory's 1855 boundary survey commission, who claimed to have seen a jaguar near Guadalupe Canyon in the Peloncillo Mountains near the present boundaries between Arizona, New Mexico, Chihuahua, and Sonora. C. B. R. Kennerly (1856), in his zoological summary of the commission's work, concluded that:

> This large cat, so common in southwestern Texas, especially along the lower Rio Grande, is rarely seen so far north as El Paso del Norte. The only individual observed by our party west of the latter place was seen in the Sierra Madre, near the Guadalupe Canyon. However, we were assured by many persons of Santa Cruz (a Sonoran border village just south of Lochiel, Arizona) that it was very common near that village, in the valley of the river of the same name.

In 1859 B. J. D. Irwin, a military doctor assigned to Fort Buchanan on Sonoita Creek, included the "leopard" in his comprehensive list of southern Arizona's wildlife (Davis 1982). However, the astute Elliot Coues, another military naturalist who was working out of Fort Whipple, farther north near Prescott, never heard of anyone encountering a jaguar in Arizona.

Not all of the early jaguar chroniclers in Arizona were military men. Phocian Way, a young prospector, reported that his partner, Mr. Fuller, killed a "tiger" while they were deer hunting in the Santa Rita Mountains during the summer of 1858 (Davis 1982).

Jaguars, or Mexican leopards, as the Americans often called them, were also being reported from Sonora. While pursuing Geronimo in the Espinazo del Diablo between the Ríos Haros (Aros) and Satachi (Bavispe) during the winter of 1885–1886, Captain Marion P. Maus of the U.S. Army jumped a "leopard that bounded away with a shriek. It was spotted and seemed as large as a tiger" (Carmony and Brown 1992).

By the late 1880s the jaguar was beginning to feel the wrath of Anglo-Americans as well as Mexican settlers. A July 31, 1890, article in Tucson's *Arizona Daily Star* reported: "The skin of the ferocious animal killed by Phil Askins, in Greenback Valley recently, was brought into Globe by his partner, Chas. Bouguot, and placed on exhibition at the post office, where it was greatly admired. The animal, undoubtedly a jaguar, is the largest and fiercest of the cat species, closely resembling a leopard, and a native of South America." For years afterward, the spring near where this animal was killed was known as Leopard Springs. The spring later became known as Lion Springs, but is now labeled on the Tonto National Forest map as Mud Springs—each change indicating a decline in the area's special nature. Jaguars must have been scarce in central Arizona, however, as a later newspaper account noted that Phil Askins had trapped more than 100 lions during his career, but only one jaguar.

With the arrival of the transcontinental railroads in the 1880s, there were now enough people in Arizona and New Mexico Territories that professional predator and bounty hunters could find a ready market for any jaguar hides that came their way. Often the sale of one of these pelts increased the animal's publicity. Herbert Brown, a newspaperman and Arizona's first resident naturalist, wrote a letter to Dr. R. W. Shufeldt in April 1902 stating:

> I send you the photograph of a very interesting animal [Figure 41] which was killed in the Rincon Mountains, about twenty-five miles east of Tucson, on the 16th of March last; it was killed by two Mexican scalp hunters. They were in the Rincons, above the Cebadilla, when their dogs found the trail of what appeared to be a very large California lion. After a short run the animal was overtaken, and two dogs were killed in the mix-up that followed. It was finally driven into a cave, smoked out and killed. . . . It measured six feet seven inches from the point of the nose to the base of the tail, and nearly ten feet from tip of nose to tip of tail, nineteen inches around the forearm and twenty-six and a half inches around the head. In the skull you will notice that the lower right canine has been broken off, but otherwise the teeth are in perfect condition. The skin and skull are in possession of William C. Brown, of Tucson, to whom I am indebted for measurements and [the] photograph. The animal was a male and very fat.

Herbert Brown went on the express his opinion as to the jaguar's status in Arizona:

> I do not think the habitat of this jaguar (Felis onca) has ever been credited to Arizona; but you will I think, agree with me that it is fairly well established. Within the last few years several have been killed in Southern Arizona. One

Figure 41. Large male jaguar killed in the Rincon Mountains, Arizona, in 1902. The setting is the porch of C. O. Brown's saloon in downtown Tucson, and the girl perched on the jaguar is Brown's daughter Caroline. Photograph 51506, courtesy of the Arizona Historical Society, Tucson.

was killed in the Chiricahuas, one in Baboquivaris, and one near Globe. Of the last there were two together, but only one was secured. Another is known to frequent a small range of rocky hills about five miles north of the Tortolita Mountains; it was last seen on the ninth of March, and a determined effort is shortly to be made to get it. There are numerous other places in which it has been taken, but I do not now definitely recall them to mind. I have seen several hides brought in by Papago Indians of animals killed in the mountains southwest of Tucson.

Jaguar hides of local origin were also being purchased and exchanged in New Mexico. The biologist Vernon Bailey (1931) was shown a "beautiful skin" of a jaguar in the home of Governor Otero in Santa Fe. The cat had been killed the previous year (1901) in Otero County, made into a rug, and presented to him. The jaguar's principal enemies, however, were the ranchers and homesteaders who were then waging a battle with predators in an effort to reduce losses to their livestock.

Ranchers and Homesteaders

Stockmen and their agents took a significant percentage of the jaguars reported killed in Arizona and New Mexico during the first quarter of the twentieth century (Table 1). Many ranchmen in those days were, in reality, small homesteaders, and the loss of even one steer or cow could be sorely felt. Thus, these stock raisers were not particularly fastidious about which predators they took. Wolves and mountain lions were the usual targets, but more than one jaguar came to a bad end at the ranchmen's hands. Some of these jaguars, such as the one shot in southeastern New Mexico in 1903 off a bull that it had presumably killed, were shot by the rancher himself. Other jaguars, including one trapped in 1900 by Nat Straw near the now-vanished settlement of Grafton in the Mogollon Mountains of New Mexico, were taken by professional hunters who were offered bounties for any predators taken. Still others were indiscriminately, if inadvertently, poisoned, as was the so-called Manning jaguar taken in New Mexico's Datil Mountains in August 1902 (Figure 42). Ned Hollister of the U.S. Biological Survey, who later inspected a mounted rug made from this animal, described the skull as belonging to an adult with well-worn teeth. Other details are summarized in Vernon Bailey's (1931) *Mammals of New Mexico:*

> Mrs. Manning had been in the habit of putting out poison to kill the predatory animals about the ranch, in the mountains 12 miles northwest of Datil and among the victims of the poisoned baits was this jaguar, which had been killing stock on the ranch for some time. It had killed 17 calves near the house during a short period before it was secured. The ranch was located at about 9,000 feet altitude in the pine and spruce timber of this exceedingly rough range of mountains. At the time Hollister was there another jaguar was supposed to be at large in the general neighborhood.

Usually, however, the rancher had some help, if not from a professional bounty hunter, from one or more of his neighbors, some of whom kept a few hounds or specialized in trapping. Thus, even though a number of jaguars were trapped, several were also trailed down with the aid of dogs and shot by houndsmen. At least one of these animals, the so-called Hands jaguar, required both methods before being brought to justice.

For some time cattle and horses were being killed in various places on the west side of the Chiricahua Mountains by what was thought to be a

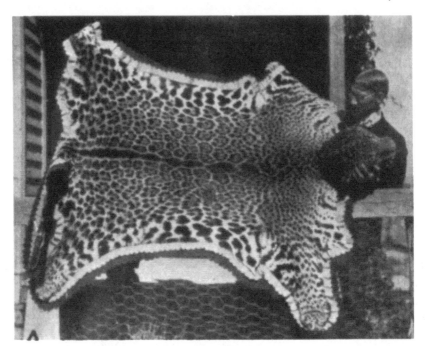

Figure 42. Pelt of a jaguar poisoned during the summer of 1902 in the Datil Mountains, New Mexico. Photograph from Bailey's (1931) *Mammals of New Mexico.*

mountain lion. Then, on January 6, 1912, a cow and a calf were killed and partially eaten on a small ranch in Bonita Canyon in what is now Chiricahua National Monument. The owner, Tommy Stafford, set a bear trap at the site of the kills in an attempt to catch the cat, which he did, but the animal was so strong that it escaped, taking the 19-lb (8.6-kg) trap with him. After tracking the animal for some distance out of the canyon, Stafford lost the trail. Afraid that he was going to lose the cat, he went to the nearby Hilltop Mine to ask for help from his friend and neighbor, E. J. "John" Hands, who had some lion dogs. The big cat proved to be elusive, however, and several days passed before Hands cut fresh sign, again in Bonita Canyon. After Hands followed the cat's tracks for most of the day and traveled some distance, it began to snow. Dusk was coming on, and Hands decided to abandon the chase and try again in the morning with the help of his brothers, Percy and Frank. The freshly fallen snow helped, and on January 12, 1912, the men followed the animal into a small cave. Peering into the darkness, Percy crawled into the cave on his hands and knees and saw a full-grown jaguar resting from his week-long ordeal of dragging the huge trap. When the wakened cat rattled the chain from less than 4 ft away, the man quickly retreated. After a short consultation as to what to do, all three men sidled into the cave, and when the jaguar lowered his head, Frank shot him.

The jaguar was taken down to Riggs settlement in Sulphur Springs Valley, where the skinned animal was photographed in the corral. Regarded as highly unusual, the Hands brothers' catch created quite a stir, and people motored in from miles around to see an "authentic leopard." Surprisingly, even though the animal was mentioned in the local paper, John Hands's diary, and the memoirs of the Riggs family history, no one actually stated the animal's sex.

Hands had the hide mounted with the skull inside the head, as was the custom of the day, and the teeth show the animal to be an old one. In 1932 Hands donated the hide to the Arizona State Museum in Tucson, but it was not destined to remain there. The hide was later transferred to a small museum of Southwestern artifacts in Portal, Arizona. That the hide is still there is somewhat of a miracle: The museum was broken into and most of the exhibits stolen or broken, with only the jaguar being returned. A sharp-eyed deputy sheriff found it in the local landfill and remembered where he had previously seen it. Although somewhat the worse for wear, the hide remains in the custody of Ted Troller, who kindly allowed us to photograph it along with the grave of the man who tracked the animal down (Figure 43).

Although the last jaguar in New Mexico had been killed in 1909, freelance predator hunters continued to take the occasional jaguar in Arizona for another 50 years. Some of these men were paid on a retainer basis, and others were paid on the basis of what they caught—one such hunter supposedly killed a female jaguar on the South Rim of the Grand Canyon in 1932. At least one professional hunter was employed by a rancher who liked to claim any predatory animals taken as his own. Working on America's first official Thanksgiving Day in 1939, Floyd "Red" Harris and his dogs trailed and dispatched a big male jaguar in Ramanote Canyon in the Sierra Atascosa (Figure 44). Although Red wasn't about to let his employer claim credit for killing the horsemeat-laden jaguar, the rancher nevertheless took its hide and skull as his right of the manor born.

Another more-or-less professional hunter, Mr. Lavern West, formerly of Forestdale, Arizona, hunted lions and bears on the White River Apache Indian Reservation from 1916 until the mid-1970s. West, an Apache tribal member, hunted at various times for clients, the Apache tribe, and the U.S. government. West killed at least one jaguar and possibly others. When

Figure 43. John Hands's grave and the pelt of the jaguar he helped kill at Portal in the Chiricahua Mountains, Arizona.

interviewed on the evening of August 10, 2000, the 102-year-old man could only recall killing a lot of both species. ¿Quien sabe? His daughter, Charyl Lynn Merino, claimed that West had brought home both lions and tigers but that all of the hides had been sold or given away. Unfortunately, we cannot verify their statements because, any family photographs and memorabilia have been burned by his Apache wife's family as befits their cultural tradition.

The use of such hunters continues, the last ones to legally kill a jaguar in Arizona were Ted Ferguson and Sewell Goodwin, who helped kill a jaguar on the Ciénega Ranch in Cochise County in 1960, an account of which is included in the section on hunting stories in this chapter. How many other jaguars were taken by these semiprofessional volunteers is difficult to say, but it is likely that at least some of their kills have gone unrecorded. This is especially true for the years prior to 1925.

Figure 44. Floyd "Red" Harris and a male jaguar taken on November 23, 1939, in the Sierra Atascosa, Arizona. Photograph courtesy of Red Harris and John Myrmo.

Although the Arizona and New Mexico territorial and state legislatures had at various times authorized the payment of bounties on predatory animals, thus freeing the stockmen of this burden, at no time were county or state bounties paid for jaguars. Jaguars were always relatively rare in these two states, as indicated by the fact that bounties were paid at various times on mountain lions, bobcats, wolves, coyotes, and even on prairie dogs, but never on "tigers," "leopards," "Mexican leopards," or "American leopards," as was the case in Texas (Appendix 1).

Thanks to the political lobbying of J. Stokely Ligon and the U.S. Biological Survey, ranchers and homesteaders were assisted in their predator control efforts after 1915 by the U.S. government. Determined to prove its worth, the Predatory Animal and Rodent Control (PARC) branch of the U.S. Biological Survey set out to rid the West of wolves, mountain lions, and other noxious animals. The agency's motto was to "bring them in no matter how," and a variety of means were employed, including hunting with hounds, trapping, and even setting out baits laced with strychnine and other poisons. There were also a number of state predator agents hired from time to time, but, like the private bounty hunters, their deeds have gone largely unchronicled.

Figure 45. John "Judge" Windes and a male jaguar killed with PARC agent Frank Colcord in the Patagonia Mountains of Arizona in 1932 or 1933. Photograph courtesy of the John Windes family.

One advantage of having the U.S. government field professional trappers and houndsmen was that the agency directed its agents to record any jaguars captured and to send the pelts and skulls to the U.S. National Museum. At least six predator control agents did so, and these skulls and their measurements are now valuable sources of information. Three of these jaguars were taken in traps, one of which is the only female from the United States in a museum collection. Another one, a male taken with dogs, became the type specimen from which the *arizonensis* subspecies was described, and two others were poisoned (Table 1). One PARC animal that apparently failed to make its way to Washington was a male taken with dogs by agent Frank Colcord in 1932 or 1933 (Figure 45). According to the Windes family history, John Windes was asked if he wanted to accompany Colcord on a mountain lion hunt in the Patagonia Mountains, where ranchers had recently reported suffering from lion depredations. Dudley jumped at the chance, especially when he was promised first shot at any cat the dogs managed to tree. What neither man dreamed was that the next cat to be treed would be a male jaguar. When the dogs' barks sounded a treed animal, Frank, who like all PARC employees in Arizona had always hoped to someday kill a jaguar, was anxious to shoot the cat.

Figure 46. Skin of what appears to be a young jaguar killed by homesteaders on the Bar FK Ranch in Rincon Valley, Arizona, 1922. Photograph courtesy of Louis Barassci and Theodore Knipe Jr.

But Dudley reminded him, "Frank, you promised me first shot." Dudley then promptly shot the jaguar in the shoulder, knocking it out of the tree. The jaguar was only wounded, however, and ran off on three legs, requiring them to shoot it again. Dudley had the jaguar's skin mounted, but three months later Frank came to him and said that he would have to turn over the hide because the government required all U.S. Biological Survey personnel to send any jaguar skulls and hides to the National Museum. Because the dogs that treed the jaguar were Colcord's, Frank reasoned that the jaguar hide belonged to him and the U.S. government. Nonetheless, the skull of the jaguar in question is not included in the U.S. National Museum's list of specimens, and it appears that neither the skull nor hide ever made it to Washington.

It is unfortunate that more borderland jaguar hides and skulls have not found their way into museums (Figure 46). Three of the Arizona specimens are within the top ten North American jaguars in the Boone and Crockett record book, and it would be interesting to know if these *norteños* were, on average, larger than those in Sonora or elsewhere in Mexico. Now, without an adequate sample size, we will probably never know the answer to this question.

Sportsmen and Jaguars

> Hunting *tigres* in southern Arizona would be seeking a needle
> in the proverbial haystack, but as soon as you cross the Mexi-
> can boundary you begin to run into spots of *tigre* country.
> Jack O'Connor (1939) *Game in the Desert*

Hunting deer and other big game as an avocation rather than to
fulfill a need did not really take hold in the United States until after the
turn of the twentieth century. But by the time Congress approved state-
hood for Arizona and New Mexico in 1912, a substantial number of citi-
zens were enjoying enough leisure time to consider themselves sportsmen.
Accordingly, the first jaguar known to have been shot by a sports hunter
was in November 1913 north of the mining town of Clifton, Arizona
(Table 1). Enough jaguars were now being killed by bounty hunters, government agents, and deer hunters that the U.S. Forest Service included
"leopards" in their 1917 summary of game animals killed on the Southwest's national forests (Appendix 2). Three years later, more jaguars
(three) were reported taken on the Coronado National Forest than mule
deer (Appendix 3)! Such anomalies were not to last, however, and the
jaguar quickly resumed its status as a highly irregular entrant in the game
rolls. Deer hunters, nonetheless, continued to kill an occasional *tigre*, including a female bagged near Arivaca, Arizona, in 1949. Another male was
shot by a deer hunter in 1957—ironically, on the same mountain as the
one killed by a deer hunter in 1913. The last Arizona jaguar killed by a
sportsman, however, was a young male shot by Laurence "Mickey" McGee
while deer hunting in the Patagonia Mountains in 1965. This animal, a
small male, was the last jaguar killed legally in Arizona.

Probably the only Southwestern jaguar taken with the aid of a predator
call was killed in September 1963 by Terry Penrod near Big Lake in Arizona's White Mountains. This animal was remarkable in several other
ways—the cat was a female, her stomach contents were recorded, and she
was weighed both whole and dressed. Most unusual, however, was that the
cat was killed in spruce-fir forest at an elevation of more than 9500 feet
(2850 m). Although these circumstances aroused some suspicions as to the
cat's origins, no one ever produced any evidence to show that the animal's
presence was anything but natural. A male jaguar killed on the nearby
White Mountain Apache Indian Reservation the following year by a government predator control agent also spoke to the Penrod cat's legitimacy.

By the 1920s, reductions in private and public bounty payments, coupled with the hiring of government hunters, was having its effect on freelance predator hunters. Feeding a pack of trained dogs throughout the year was an expensive proposition, and most hunters also had a small ranch to help make ends meet. Also, chasing lions and bears with dogs was an adventure that desk-bound hunters from the East would gladly pay to enjoy. Given even a modest bounty or retainer to hunt predators and a well-heeled dude to shoot them, a man could still make a living as a professional predator hunter. Although mountain lions were the usual quarry and could be hunted year-round, every houndsman dreamed of someday catching a jaguar. The problem, of course, was that jaguars had never been numerous enough in the United States that someone could actually hunt for one.

No less a houndsman than Ben Lilly unsuccessfully pursued any report of a jaguar that came his way. The Lee brothers, arguably the region's foremost lion hunters, also yearned for a jaguar. They knew, however, that jaguars were just not predictable enough to hunt in Arizona. Accordingly, in 1935, they began hunting jaguars in Sonora, where they had immediate success (see their story below). Before long, all of the big-time Arizona lion chasers were going to Mexico to try their luck at a jaguar. No guide or client ever intentionally set out to kill a jaguar in Arizona and did so—at least not until the 1950s.

Eyebrows were therefore rightfully raised when three jaguars were taken on guided hunts in Arizona and another one near Marfa, Texas, in the 1950s. All of these fortunate hunters had employed the same guide, an experienced and wide-ranging lion and bear hunter who also had a hunting camp in what was then British Honduras. According to his onetime partner, the two of them smuggled more than one jaguar in and out of Mexico, having some incredible adventures in the process. Suspicions intensified, however, when the senior partner was convicted of transporting a mountain lion across the Idaho state line to be released for one of his clients. There were other suspicious circumstances. At least one taxidermist noted that an "Arizona jaguar" that he was to mount had soiled itself. Only a cat kept in a cage, he said, did that. Enough said. No jaguar taken in the United States on a guided hunt specifically for jaguars can be considered legitimate. The odds against such a happening are just too great.

Although the Arizona Game and Fish Commission made the jaguar a protected animal in 1969, this new regulation attracted little attention—at least until November 16, 1971, when two teenaged duck hunters sneaking

Figure 47. Bob Farley and his jaguar in 1999. Note the separate head mount.

up on a stock tank a few miles north of the Mexican border came upon a full-grown male jaguar. Naturally, they shot it. Blinded by a charge of shot fired from only a few yards away, the jaguar slunk into a nearby cavern, where it was promptly dispatched. When the plucky lads were later cited by the local wildlife manager, an unhappy legal imbroglio ensued. The state had no chance for making a case. Not only was the judge a relative of one of the boys, no less a jaguar expert than Dale Lee testified that the boys had done the safe and prudent thing and acted in self-defense. Both defendants were quickly acquitted, and the hide promptly returned, even though the head had somehow been cut off in the interim, as befits a true borderland *bandito* (Figure 47). As for the state's case, the jaguar's skull was ordered to be deposited in the University of Arizona mammal collection, from where it has since disappeared.

Fifteen years passed before another jaguar was to make Arizona's newspapers. In December 1986, a rumor that a local rancher had killed a jaguar began circulating around the hamlet of Willcox in the southeastern portion of the state. Several people had supposedly seen the animal's carcass, and there were reports that photographs had been taken. But, despite a reward offered by the Arizona Game and Fish Department that exceeded $4000, no one came forth with information sufficient to obtain a search

Figure 48. Jaguar killed in December 1986 near Willcox, Arizona. Photograph courtesy of the Arizona Game and Fish Department.

warrant or issue a citation. A plea bargain agreement disintegrated when the killer refused to reveal the whereabouts of the jaguar's hide. "It was," he reportedly said, "the greatest trophy of my life." Even though the animal was said to be a male and of no biological consequence, conservationists were outraged. Their cries for a federal investigation were stymied, however, by the fact that only jaguars south of the U.S.-Mexico border were then protected under the Endangered Species Act.

What the general public did not know was that a federal investigation was already in progress. State and federal agents were setting the suspects up for a sting operation targeting illegal guiding and the taking of big game animals out of season. Finally, after several delays, John Klump and Tim Haas were convicted of illegally taking a bighorn sheep—a class 6 felony. Among the evidence seized during the investigation were a jaguar hide, a mounted jaguar, and two ocelots. Diaries and photographs (Figure 48) indicated that the jaguar pelt was from an animal killed with the aid of dogs in the Dos Cabezas Mountains east of Willcox, and that the other spotted cats had been illegally taken in the Mexican state of Campeche. Because foreign jaguars are listed as endangered and are also protected under the Convention on International Trade in Endangered Species, the U.S. Fish and Wildlife Service filed federal charges against both men.

Although they had originally plead guilty before a federal judge, in 1995 the defendants were allowed to change their plea to not guilty. The felony charges were then dismissed by U.S. District Judge Richard Bilby on the grounds of entrapment. The evidence of photographs, mounts, and hides was also, therefore, inadmissible—a decision that was upheld even after being appealed by the U.S. Department of Justice. Thus, neither of Arizona's two protected jaguars were deemed to have been illegally taken, illustrating the difficulty of obtaining convictions for killing endangered species that were considered potentially dangerous or damaging.

These court cases made the jaguars photographed by houndsmen Warner Glenn and Jack Childs in 1996 that much more remarkable. That these animals, both of which are discussed in the introduction, had been bayed and treed without being killed indicated a change in the attitude of at least some lion-hunting Arizonans. The stage was now set, some reasoned, for a general change in the management of these animals. Perhaps it was time for the jaguar to make a comeback. The problem, however, was not political but biological. Neither a change in attitudes nor a change in regulations would suffice. In fact, there was not a jaguar population in Arizona to protect. The first order of business was to find out where Warner Glenn's and Jack Childs's cats had come from. If that could be determined, the problem of how populations of borderland jaguars might be saved or increased might be solved.

Jaguars in Northern Sonora

> At Agua Fria Ranch in Sonora, the Americans keep a professional lion-hunter, with a pack of trained dogs. Unless their prowling raids were continuously resisted, the wild beasts would soon overrun the ranch. Last year this hunter killed over 50 animals, including lions, tigers, and wildcats.
>
> G. Simplich (1919)

There are numerous eighteenth-century references to jaguars in Sonora, mostly by explorers and European missionaries who primarily saw the animals as threats to livestock raising. Father Luis Velarde, for example, in his 1716 *Relación of Pimería Alta,* accurately lists the fauna present between the thirtieth and thirty-fourth parallels as living in a temperate climate and consisting of "tigers, lions, bears, wild cats, wolves, foxes, coyotes, mountain sheep, deer, hares, rabbits, and other creatures" (Wyllys 1931). Another Jesuit missionary, Father Philipp Segesser referred to a lion in his descriptions of Papagueria, which he said was really a leopard, a creature that harmed cattle. He also referred to depredations being caused by a tiger around Tecoripa, Sonora, as early as 1739. And so it went. Jaguars and lions, while recognized as hindrances to stock raising, were regarded as a constant toll that must be paid, regardless of whether preventive measures were applied. Should losses be especially severe, predator control measures such as trapping, following up animals with dogs, and even poisoning might be resorted to; if losses were low, this good fortune was attributed to good weather and *gracias a Dios.* Predator hunting was a part-time occupation conducted to relieve a specific problem—a problem that was usually considered solved with the sale of the offending animal's pelt.

American ranchers in Mexico, of which there were a number prior to the 1910 revolution, had a different attitude. Predators were not regarded merely as a cost of doing business, their elimination was considered a long-term operating expense. Accordingly, many of the larger operations, such as the huge RO Ranch, hired predator trappers on a full-time basis. Very often these professional hunters were also Americans, some of them coming out of Texas, but also from the Mormon colonies in Chihuahua and Sonora. How effective these professionals were is difficult to say, because we have no records of their activities. Some of these men appear to have been quite good at their trade, however, and probably impacted jaguar populations at least locally (Figure 49). Whatever effect they might have had was short-lived, however, because the large American holdings were eventually replaced by Mexican ranches after the revolution ended in the early 1920s. By the 1950s, few if any ranches in Sonora were being managed by Americans, and the Sonorans were generally back to handling their own predator problems, as they had throughout most of their history.

Jaguars were still legal to hunt in Mexico, however. As early as in the 1920s and 1930s a few predator trappers took to guiding American *ricos.* Not all of these guides were local men. In the 1930s two enterprising houndsmen and outfitters from Tucson, Arizona, Dale and Clell Lee, decided they wanted to catch a jaguar and maybe find a jaguar hunting locale

Figure 49. Leonard Lee "Bud" Davis with jaguar and other cat hides taken in the late 1940s or early 1950s on the RO Ranch in Sonora, Mexico. Photograph courtesy of Charyn Davis.

Figure 50. Dale Lee and two jaguar hides taken in 1935 near the junction of Ríos Aros and Bavispe. Photograph 2113, courtesy of the Arizona Historical Society, Tucson.

Figure 51. Male jaguar taken in 1963 by Alfonso Barragán in the Sierra Frentón, Sonora. Photograph courtesy of Eli Hernández.

for their clients. A man named Baldy Hobbs, who was married to a Sonoran woman, suggested they try hunting where the Ríos Aros, Bavispe, and Yaqui come together. This they did, bagging eight jaguars there between 1935 and 1937 (Table 2, Figure 50). Other Americans also tried their hand at guiding, but jaguar hunting in the hot uplands of central Sonora was a tough proposition for guides, dogs, and clients. The Lees soon moved on to Sinaloa, where jaguars were more common, and later, in the 1940s, they discovered the Agua Brava swamplands along the coast of Nayarit, where jaguars were not only numerous but a lot easier to come by. Sonora's short history as a jaguar-hunting Mecca had come to a close almost as soon as it began.

After 1950 or so, jaguar hunting in Sonora was again essentially in the hands of the local ranchers, who concentrated their attention on depredating animals (Figure 51). Lions were the main problem, but a *tigre* might become a local nuisance; also, a jaguar would often be taken

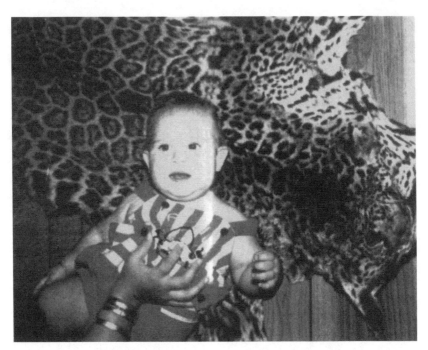

Figure 52. The pelt of a more than twelve-year-old female jaguar killed in the Sierra de los Chinos near Sahuaripa, Sonora, in 1995.

incidental to trapping for a *león*. As had been the case with Arizona's ranchers and homesteaders during the first half of the twentieth century, the steel trap was the usual weapon of choice. Nonetheless, as cat hunting became more sophisticated, a local cadre of houndsmen often developed. And, should either a trapper or a houndsmen show promise as a lion hunter, his services would be requested throughout the local ranching community. If conventional methods proved inconvenient for whatever reason, the carcass of a cow or other animal might also be poisoned. When a jaguar was taken, its hide was usually kept as a souvenir or purchased locally (Figures 52–54). Sport hunting of jaguars was virtually nonexistent, and no pelts are known to have found their way to the international fur market.

The important question was not only if jaguars were still being killed in Sonora, but how many? To answer this question, we decided to revisit the Lee's old hunting grounds and see if any *tigres* were still down there. If they were, we reasoned, the cats would be taking livestock and people would be killing them—never mind that jaguars have been protected in Mexico since 1986. Sonorans have always been isolated from the national bureaucracy in Mexico City and play pretty well by their own rules.

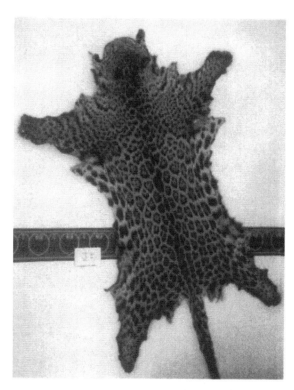

Figure 53. The hide of a female jaguar that was reportedly lactating when killed near the boundary of the *municipios* of Huasabas and Divisaderos, Sonora, in 1996.

The problem was that ranchers and predator hunters were not going to rush up and tell a *gringo* and a *chilango* about any jaguars they had recently killed. So we adopted a strategy that Texas trapper Roy T. McBride had developed for searching out the last Mexican wolves in Chihuahua and Durango, a strategy previously found to be helpful in locating vampire bat roosts in southern Sonora.

The state of Sonora is divided into seventy-two *municipios,* each having an *asociación ganadera,* or livestock sanitary office, that coordinates ranching activities (Map 7). Incidence of predation by mountain lions and jaguars would be common knowledge to these officials, and they would know which ranchers were having problems with these animals and what was being done about them. Because we had no affiliation with any government agency and were genuinely interested in any predator problems that ranchers were having, we hoped that these officials would tell us of any jaguar occurrences. Hopefully, after winning their trust, we would then be introduced to the local ranchers and predator hunters, who, in turn, would show us the skulls and hides of any cats they had killed. Because reports of jaguar sightings are unreliable, we would only plot the

Figure 54. A young male jaguar killed near San Javier, Sonora, in 1998.

localities of dead jaguars that had ben photographed or whose hides or skulls we had seen.

Our success exceeded all our expectations. One report led to another and that to another. As we moved from one *municipio* to the next, a network of cooperators gradually evolved. Livestock officials, ranchmen, vaqueros, hunters, trappers, and hide tanners all had stories to tell of their adventures with *leones* and *tigres*. Eventually people began showing us the hides and sometimes the skulls. Anyone who had ever had an encounter with a jaguar seemed impelled to tell about it.

Sonora is a big, rugged state, much of it relatively empty. No jaguar network would allow us to document the presence or absence of jaguars

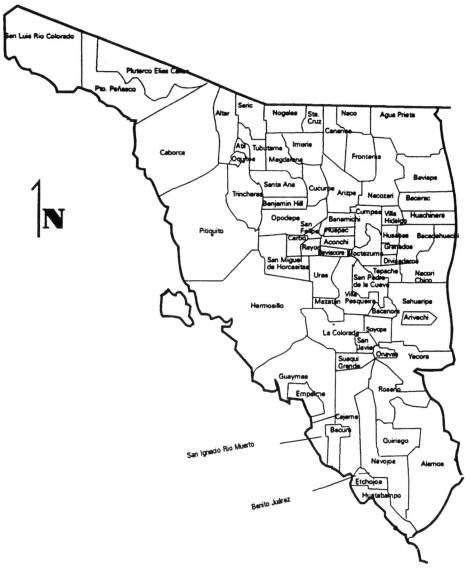

Map 7. Sonora's *municipios*.

over the entire state. But we were aided by the generally friendly population and a lot of good luck. One example or our luck was the chance glimpse of a jaguar photograph being developed in a camera store in the resort city of Mazatlán in the neighboring state of Sinaloa. Asked for details, the clerk said he had killed the jaguar the previous year on a ranch

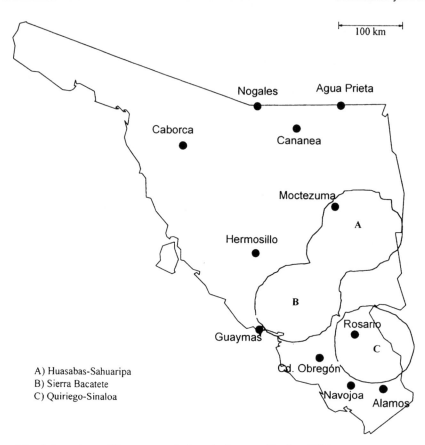

Map 8. Locations of jaguar populations in Sonora, Mexico, 2000.

only 20 mi east of town. This report led to other reports of jaguars in the same area, convincing us that a population is still extant in the rugged *barrancas* connecting northern Sinaloa and southern Sonora. Other reports and photographs indicate a less exploited jaguar population in the Sierra Bacatete and adjoining lands in the Yaqui Indian country in southwestern Sonora (Map 8).

Most of the jaguars that we have documented over the last five years have been within a 50-mi radius of the junction of the Ríos Aros and Yaqui—the area discovered by the Lee brothers in the 1930s. This population, which we call the Huasabas-Sahuaripa population after two main villages in the area, is almost certainly the source of the jaguars that recently found their way into Arizona. The center of this population is 140 mi south of where Warner Glenn photographed his jaguar in the Peloncillo

Mountains and 200 mi from where Jack Childs treed his jaguar in the Baboquivari Mountains. Both distances are within the documented dispersal range of male mountain lions. It seems reasonable that a northern jaguar could travel a similar distance.

So far we have accumulated more than 136 jaguar records from Sonora, mostly south of the thirtieth parallel (Table 2). Although the Huasabas-Sahuaripa population has been exploited for many years, it still contains females and cubs, and, at least until recently, appeared to be self-sustaining. Unfortunately this situation may now be changing. Not only were an uncomfortably large number of females removed during the 1998–1999 drought period, but at least two animals appeared to have been killed by carcasses poisoned with a lethal agricultural pesticide. After all these years, it would be tragic to lose this, the northernmost breeding population of jaguars. If this population disappears, there won't be any more visiting jaguars for Warner Glenn or anybody else to photograph.

Other statistics are even more alarming. At least fifty jaguars have been killed during the last decade, and we know of at least six that were taken in 1999, including four that were either cubs or lactating females. All three of the jaguar populations that we have identified are exploited to some degree, but the Huasabas-Sahuaripa population appears to be in the most imminent danger.

Although killing a jaguar has always been a matter of pride on either side of the border, the motivation is more economically driven in Sonora, where killing a jaguar is often merely a response to a problem. The simple truth is that jaguars are still being killed in Sonora because cattle are more important to Sonorans than large cats. Thus, it is more difficult for someone in Sonora to let a jaguar go as Warner Glenn and Jack Childs did in Arizona. More is needed in Sonora than a heightened sense of environmental awareness.

Most of the jaguars killed in Sonora are in their prime and appear to be in good health. But cattle range virtually everywhere and are now a regular part of the jaguar's diet, even in those areas where white-tailed deer and javelina are common. Semiwild cattle are part of the Sonoran thornscrub ecosystem, and because livestock management in the rugged Sonoran backcountry has changed little since the days of the Jesuit missionaries, cattle will continue to be fed upon by both mountain lions and jaguars (Figure 55). And, as long as cattle are being killed, both species of big cat will continue to be trapped, hunted, and poisoned. The only way to reduce these depredations is to introduce more intensive livestock management

Figure 55. A jaguar feeding on a cow in east-central Sonora.

practices, such as confining cows and calves to particular pastures and fencing all of the cattle out of the rougher bluffs and canyons. But changing 300-year-old practices are not going to be easy.

There are other threats to Sonora's jaguars. Although the Huasabas-Sahuaripa area's remoteness and low human density have made it a jaguar stronghold for sixty years, changes are rumored to be on the way. These changes include plans to build additional dams on the Ríos Bavispe and Yaqui and perhaps on the Aros as well. Such dams would be sure to bring new roads and increased exploitation of the region's natural resources. What is now a two-day trip from such population centers as Hermosillo and Nogales would be reduced to half a day.

Another potential threat is a plan for a series of open-pit mines in the very heart of the Huasabas-Sahuaripa area. One has only to look at the existing copper mine at Nacozari in the Sierra Madera to the east to imagine the impact of such an operation. Disposal of enormous quantities of spoil and the construction of massive settling ponds have already negated many of the wildlife values of the once extensive Sierra Madera. A similar operation in the Lee brothers' old hunting grounds would be a disaster for jaguars.

Hunting Jaguars

The jaguar is constantly pursued and hunted in all possible ways because of his harmfulness.

Brehm (1895) *Animals of the World*

Tables 1 and 2 show that the jaguars taken in the Southwestern borderlands during the twentieth century were about equally divided between those trapped, brought to bay with dogs, or just come upon and shot. The same is true in both Arizona and Sonora, although the use of steel traps was the more common method of take in the United States prior to 1950, dogs being used more successfully during the last half of the century. In addition, at least five jaguars were reported to have been poisoned in Arizona, and we know of several animals in Sonora that were also killed in this manner. Poisons were not used more in the United States largely due to the incompatibility of using dogs to hunt lions in those areas where lethal predacides had been deployed. If, as many Sonorans believe, jaguars are more prone to return to a poisoned bait than lions, this method may have been more destructive to jaguars than anyone realized. Poisoned animals are often difficult to find and usually go unreported. One can only guess how many jaguars might have been killed during the heyday of the use of strychnine in the years prior to World War II and the deployment of compound 1080 in the 1950s and 1960s.

Whereas staking out a goat or other potential prey animal is a common jaguar hunting technique in Central and South America, to our knowledge this has not been employed along the border. The same is also true of still-hunting over a dead cow or other carcass, although several jaguars have been shot while feeding on dead animals. In 1949 Walter Noon shot a jaguar that was intently watching him clean a buck white-tailed deer, and there are several reports of jaguars being shot while feeding on livestock that they had either just killed or were in the process of killing (Table 1). Jaguars in both Arizona and Sonora have stood their ground to the point that they have reportedly been killed with rocks.

The only person we know to have successfully called in a borderland jaguar is Terry Penrod, who used a commercial predator call to take a female jaguar in the White Mountains (Table 1). Using a jaguar call to elicit calls and locate jaguars is a technique widely used elsewhere, however. In fact, Dale Lee and other jaguar hunters used jaguar calls with some success in almost every other area than in the rugged and arid mountains of Sonora. This was especially true in the mangrove forests surrounding the Agua Brava in the *Marismas Nacionales* where both American and Mexican hunter-guides took good numbers of jaguars in the 1950s and 1960s.

Jaguar calls can be made out of a gourd, a steer horn, or even an old peach can (Figure 56). A piece of skin is stretched over an opening in the gourd, horn, or can. Another hole is then cut in the bottom. A waxed cord

Figure 56. Carlos
López González using
a jaguar call.

of braided horsehair (native beeswax is said to be best) is then securely fas-
tened to the center of the stretched skin and drawn down through the
lower opening. When the cord is pulled (and with a little practice and per-
severance), the friction created as the cord slips through the fingers can
make the *uh, uh, uh* sound of a jaguar on the prowl. Although the device
can supposedly call in a jaguar, the primary purpose of using a call is to locate an animal for the dogs to start in the morning.

Most jaguars were and are taken through the use of trained lion
hounds. Taking these big cats in this manner is no easy task, however. In
addition to the hundreds of hours of dog-training involved, the hunter
must withstand hours in the saddle and be able to negotiate the steepest
and most brush-choked country imaginable. Most importantly, the hunter
must be able to interpret the slightest bit of sign and determine which
strategy to employ. The following jaguar hunting stories have been se-
lected as illustrative, not only of the techniques involved, but the mind-set
and dedication necessary to bring a hunt to a successful conclusion.

Figure 57. Promotional photograph featuring a jaguar killed by the Lee brothers in Sonora, Mexico, in the late 1930s.

Hunting Stories

We got to counting up the days, and it was eighteen days, I believe, so we'd hunted four days overtime. But, in that length of time, we had gotten one ocelot, a bobcat, a mountain lion, and a jaguar, which were about all the cats they had in that country.

Dale Lee's "A Guaranteed Jaguar," as told to
Robert L. McCurdy (1979)

Jaguar hunting stories have been an integral part of every jaguar hunt for as long as people have been pursuing these big cats. We have read perhaps two dozen borderland stories that have made it into the literature and heard numerous others. In so doing, two things become noticeable— how repetitious these stories can become, and how this repetition can lead to the teller embellishing the story. In fact, many accounts are just that— stories. Other accounts are more substantial and contain valuable information, either in the actual narrative or between the lines.

The earliest borderlands story we have come across is one published in 1889 in *The Great Divide* of Denver, Colorado (Vol. 1, no. 4). Supposedly taking place in Dolores Canyon in Chihuahua, the tale involves Paul Gillet and his miner friends coming upon a cave full of golden *tigres*. After some miscalculations they eventually dispatch no fewer than five of the beasts, selling the adult pelts for $30 apiece and the hides of two young animals for $20 each. Unfortunately, the story is too vague and implausible to be taken at face value.

By far the best of the early stories is one by John M. Phillips (1913), entitled "Transplanting the Jungle King." This exciting account describes the successful effort to photograph and obtain a pair of jaguars for the Cleveland Natural History Museum in 1910. Unfortunately, the action takes place not in the Southwestern borderlands, but in analogous habitats in the semi-arid brushlands around the town of Ebano on the Tamaulipas-Veracruz border.

Western writer J. S. P. Brown's novel *The Forests of the Night* tells of an Indian man's pursuit of a jaguar *(El Yoco)* in the vicinity of San Bernardo, Sonora. Although this well-written book paints an accurate picture of the Sonoran countryside and the lives and mores of the local people, the descriptions of *El Yoco* and his behavior are more anthropomorphic than real. Nonetheless, the habitats are accurately portrayed, and one can learn some good regional folklore. A less polished, but better and more accurate read, is *Life of the Greatest Guide* as told by Dale Lee to Robert L. McCurdy. This book is as authentic as you can get. Having known Dale personally, I can attest that he was as good a storyteller as he was a jaguar hunter, being in on 115 jaguar kills (Figure 57). The following story, republished here with the permission of Robert McCurdy, describes the Lee brothers' first attempt, in 1935, to hunt jaguars in the state of Sonora. The area involved, near the junction of the Ríos Granados (Yaqui) and Aros, is the same area where we found jaguars in 1998 and where jaguars are found today.

My First Jaguar Hunt

By Dale Lee as told to Robert McCurdy

I was twenty-seven when I made my first jaguar hunt, and it took place on the Río Yaqui. On this hunt, there was Clell, and a boy that came from Canada, from Toronto, and he was a soldier of fortune if I ever saw one. He was about my age when he came to the Chiricahuas, to Paradise, where we lived then. He made a lion hunt into the Mogollon Mountains, in New Mexico, with us, got a big lion, and in a few days, he was back, wanting to go into Mexico for a jaguar hunt.

And, golly, it was in the summertime, and we told him that it would be terrible down there that time of year. But he said he might not get to make it otherwise, and, said he would pay good money, and just take his chances on a jaguar. Then we went to Douglas and got an old fellow by the name of Baldy Hobbs. I don't remember his first name, but he was real baldheaded, and everyone called him Baldy. He'd been down in that country in Sonora, and he'd married a native girl, and had a family, but had moved back to Douglas.

Let's see, Baldy had an old Dodge, we had an old Chevrolet, and, uh, this boy from Toronto had an old Buick. Now, this boy's name was Douglas Deeks, but when he came out West, and they asked him what his name was, by golly, he said Dobe. You know this 'dobe they used to make houses out of? He said, "My name's Dobe Deeks," so everybody called him Dobe.

We started out, and went down through Nogales, down through Cananea, and worked over to a little town called Divisideros. We were going to get a pack outfit there, and pack over to the junction of the Granados and the Aros. Baldy said he had hunted jaguars several years before, and had found them in that country.

But meanwhile, the generator in this old Buick had gone bad, and Dobe wanted to get it fixed, to go to Hermosillo and get it fixed. We told him we ought to make the hunt first, but he wanted his car fixed, so he and I started out, and me speaking but very little Spanish at that time.

So we left Clell, and Baldy, and an old fellow we had cooking for us by the name of Walt Fenecom, and they were going to pack over to the river, and wait for us there, and we'd be back in three or four days. Well, lord gosh, we like to never got that old Buick there. We had to leave it, and go to Hermosillo on a truck, and then get a mechanic to come back and get this old Buick and take it in. And then the generator had to be sent to Mexico City to be rewound, and that took us eleven days.

And Clell had a fit. He had camped at the river for a few days, and then made a second trip over to pack back the whole outfit. On the eleventh day, we were coming back, and he was coming to look for us. He didn't know what had happened. I think he thought a Mexican had cut our throats or something. Anyway, we got back to the river, and got our outfit, but it was so hot we couldn't travel in the daytime. The dogs couldn't go in the hot country without tearing their pads off, so we went at night. We got up on top of this big canyon, up above the river, and the guides lost the trail. They wandered around for about three hours before we got started off again, and we were only about halfway down when it broke daylight. The sun had just broken over the hill when we hit a little saddle running down the ridge to the river. Two of the hounds got mixed up in the pack outfit, and I went down to get them, when Clell hollered at me.

"Get back up here. I found a track here that looks awful funny. I've never seen one looked like it."

We'd never seen a jaguar track, and I hurried back up to look. We knew it was some kind of big cat, knew it wasn't a lion, and figured it had to be a jaguar.

And Clell said, "We came here to run a jaguar. Let's run 'im."

Well, Dobe had gotten down the trail a ways with the rest of the outfit, so I ran down and got him. When we got back, Clell and the dogs were gone on the jaguar track.

Dobe and I took Clell's tracks up this ridge a little ways, and then it started to rim off into a deep canyon. It looked like a small Grand Canyon, and on the edge stood Clell's horse, chaps, spurs, and everything. And we could hear the hounds way down the canyon.

We piled off our horses, and took after the hounds, but when we made the bottom, we could tell the hounds were headed back up. We got on top of a great big rock, about the size of a small house, to hear which way, for sure, the hounds were running. And, by golly, they were rimming out on the same side we had come off of, but they turned back, and came down right under the rock, right by the rock we were sitting on, and on up the rim on the other side. And in a minute, they jumped.

And Clell had been coming off behind them, quite a ways back up there, and he hollered at me.

"Get after those hounds. They've jumped that thing."

And they were going right up the other wall of the canyon.

"Come on, Dobe. Let's go."

"Aw," he said. "It'll take me the rest of the day to get back to that horse."

Said, "Don't you pay any attention to me. You get on after those dogs, and I'll try to get back to the horses, and take 'em down to the river, and see if I can find camp."

So boy, I steamed out of there, and I went up over that rim just as fast as I could. When I got up on top of the canyon, I heard an old hound named Jake say, "Aaaooo," just as he went out of hearing. And that must've been two miles or more across a bunch of canyons and ridges. I started in that direction, and when I topped the ridge where I'd heard them last, I stopped to listen, and by golly, they were bayed.

I got in such a hurry, and the echo was sounding up and down, and I'd start in one direction, and yep, that was right, and then, no, they'd be another way.

That wouldn't do, so I climbed a little peak that was right there. I finally got the right direction, and started to them again. I got up fifty or seventy-five yards, and could tell they were barking in a cave. I had one of those coon hunter lights that, you know, you put the batteries on your belt, and the light on your head, and you can look, uh, you can use both hands.

So I jerked out my light, and, by golly, it opened, and all the batteries fell out. I sat down on a rock, and fooled with the light til I got it working, and as I raised up to start in the cave, I heard the brush popping in this little canyon, and here come Clell, his face red as a beet. I mean, he was just about to get overheated.

"By golly, they got 'im."

"Yeah," he says, "I hear 'em."

So we walked on up to the cave. Now, we'd been told that if a jaguar went in a cave, he'd run out and bray like a burro. We got on either side of the cave, sat down, and got ready. We both had rifles, and when the jaguar ran out to bray, we figured to do something about it.

We sat for quite a little while, and nothing happened. Of our eight hounds, five were on the outside, and only two were inside. Well, we each one wanted to kill this jaguar, the first one for any of us, and we had a dickens of an argument.

Who was going in the cave?

"Well, now listen," Clell said, "you know, I can shoot straighter than you can, so let's do this. Let's both go in there. You hold the light, and I'll do the shootin'."

He slipped in, and I slipped in right behind him. The hole went right down for ten or twelve feet, and kind of made a little room in there. One of the hounds was down on the floor, the other one back on a ledge, and they were looking towards the back of this hole. We could stand up, but only slant-wise, 'cause the cave wasn't straight up and down. It was slanted, which made for a poor position. I got the light going, and back, not back over twelve feet in the cave, through a kind of triangular opening in the rocks, we could see the jaguar's eyes and part of his head. And he was looking at us through the same opening.

"Put 'er right between his eyes," I said.

He raised up, and shot, and the dot-danged dust just flew. And my light shorted out, and goddamn, I had it, I was yanking on the wires, and pounding on it, and Clell just chambered another round, right quick, and stuck his barrel out in front of him. And nothing happened.

I got my light going, and shined back there, and there it was. The bullet had hit a rock on the left side, and splattered into the jaguar's eye. It put one eye out, and the blood was running down his head, and he was still standing there.

"By golly," I said, "you didn't do so good that first time. You better try 'er again."

So he raised up that time, and hit it right between the eyes, and the jaguar fell.

We dragged it to the floor of the cave, gutted it, and started for the river. We knew our camp was somewhere up the river, but it was so hot, we couldn't get our dogs to travel. We took them back to the cave, and stayed there all day. Just as it was getting sundown, we got them back to the river, and started walking.

We were walking up the river right brisk, and here came old Baldy on a mule, coming down the river.

"Where in the devil are you a'goin', Baldy?" we asked him.

Said, "Well, I come to look for you fellows. Got something for you to eat."

Says, "I didn't know where I's goin', but I thought you ought to be in this direction, somewhere."

Now, Baldy had told us to never hunt more than four hounds on a jaguar, 'cause the tigre'd kill them and get away. There were only a couple of hounds with us, the rest of them crippling behind us.

So we said, "By golly, Baldy, you were right." Said, "Look, we only got two dogs left."

And, boy, he started preaching us a sermon, then, about how we hadn't listened to him, and in a minute, another dog limped up. And another, and another, and Baldy slowly stopped talking.

Finally, we said, "Well, Baldy, if you take more than four hounds, it may kill 'em all, but we got a jaguar layin' in a cave yonder, and, we got the rest of the hounds. Your theory doesn't work all the time, anyway."

So we went on up the Río Granados a couple of miles, back to camp, and that was a pretty welcome sight. We were tired and hungry, but of course, very tickled, 'cause that was our first jaguar.

It was a good, grown female, and before this hunt was over, we got

Figure 58. The Total
Wreck Mine jaguar.
The men are Sewell
Goodwin
(foreground), Harry
Barnett, owner of the
La Ciénega Ranch
(standing), and Ted
Ferguson. Photograph
courtesy of Sewell
Goodwin.

another grown female and a cub, and a good lion. We had only hunted eight days, so, by golly, on our first jaguar hunt, we thought we had done pretty good.

And this hound that wasn't there, he had gone plumb back to Divisideros, back to where we'd had a camp. A Mexican got him, and brought him to our camp on the river, so we ended up with all our hounds.

Well, it was over, but we had a dickens of a time getting out. We had to go back through Hermosillo, and old Dobe went on a big toot, and spent all the money we had.

"Oh, I can get us plenty of money," he said, and went to see a banker he had known before, but the banker had gone on a vacation for two weeks. So we went to one of the big hotels, put our hounds and our truck in the patio, and charged everything. We were there for five days.

Dobe wired for money, and money came, and we headed for Nogales, but every little ways, we'd have a flat tire. The tires had gotten so bad on that old Dodge of Baldy's, and we fixed one flat after another. Finally, Dobe went into Nogales, and came back with some good tires. We had been gone just about a month, but we didn't get to hunt but eight days of that time. We thought we'd done pretty good for our first jaguar hunt.

The following accounts of a stock-killing jaguar are from an article written by W. F. Barnett, foreman of the Ciénega Ranch near Sonoita, Arizona, and a tape-recorded recollection of the same event by Sewell Goodwin, who presently lives near Glenwood, New Mexico. Originally published in the August 1961 issue of the *Arizona Cattlelog,* Barnett's article authentically relates how relentless the ranchmen pursue these cats when one of their animals has been killed. Note, too, the amount of local cooperation involved among the stockmen and their neighbors. And, as in most truthful accounts, one also learns some jaguar natural history in the process, in this case both Barnett and Goodwin describe the cat's penchant for taking calves, its tendency to seek refuge in caves or tunnels, and the nuances and difficulties of trailing one in dry weather. The jaguar was killed on July 25, 1961, and the hide is now in Goodwin's possession (Figure 58). First, we present Barnett's version.

A Jaguar Was Caught in Arizona

By W. F. Barnett

The first proof we had of this animal and his activities was when my brother Harry noticed a cow that had lost her calf. Seeing some buzzards circling over a brush thicket across the creek, he rode over and as his horse entered the brush an animal jumped out of a low place in the ground and was out of sight in an instant. It looked to him like a lion, so without further investigation he came to the ranch and reported that there was a lion on our range. We phoned John Gleason of Nogales to come and bring his dogs. He got in touch with a friend in Tucson who also had some hounds. In about 36 hours both were here with their dogs, and they picked up the trail near where the animal was first seen. However, the weather was hot and it was dusty and the dogs were unable to follow the trail. After giving up the hunt for that day we investigated the place where Harry first saw the lion and there was a freshly killed calf, and bones of another calf scattered around.

A week went by before we found anything; then there were fresh tracks, and in the meantime a neighbor, Orion Enzenberg, who has some cattle in a pasture about a mile west of the Ciénega headquarters, reported two calves missing.

We then contacted Sewell Goodwin of Sunnyside who has lion dogs. On his way here he called Ted Ferguson of Central, whose ranch is on the Gila below Safford, to come with his dogs. They arrived that night with about 15 hounds between them.

We all left the ranch early next morning and the dogs quickly picked up the track about a mile below the ranch and they followed it down the creek about 1-1/2 miles where it played out. The dogs worked hard trying to find it but the weather was so unfavorable that they had to give it up. We brought the dogs home but Harry went farther and found where the animal had dropped back to the creek three or four miles further on, so next morning they took the dogs down there, picked up the trail again and followed it out of our range, over onto Roy Semund's Empirita Ranch, but after traveling four or five miles they had to quit again on account of the weather.

After that we were all busy spraying cattle and didn't find any sign for two or three days. Then, Harry and Bailey Foster, who also works here, found fresh tracks where he had come back to his old "stomping ground," but we did not make another attempt to get him so long as the weather was dry, hoping for rain to put moisture in the ground so the dogs could work.

Finally, we got rain and our neighbor Eddie Hilton volunteered to help find fresh sign and made a date to meet Harry on the creek a certain day. Hilton and his wife rode from their ranch horseback over onto our side. On their way they climbed up to an old abandoned mine tunnel, high on the side of the ridge and found signs where [the cat] had been using the tunnel as a lair for quite a while. They then went on to the creek and found Harry following a cow that had lost her calf. Leaving the cow, they found fresh tracks where the animal came down a trail to water after it had rained the night before.

We immediately went to Sewell's ranch to tell him of our find and then called Ferguson about 3:00 P.M. They were here by dark that evening. Early next morning Harry, Hilton, Ferguson, Sewell, and above all—the dogs— easily picked up the trail where they had seen his tracks the day before. With more favorable weather conditions the dogs had no trouble following him in practically a straight line to the old tunnel. Upon arriving there, the dogs circled the mouth of the tunnel but could not pick up any trail. They split the dogs into two bunches and made a wide circle of a mile or more, without results.

Returning to the tunnel, they made torches of sticks and crawled into the tunnel but their torches burned out and they had to come out. Then Harry went back to the ranch house to get a flashlight, and he and Ted Ferguson went back in, Harry carrying Hilton's .30/30 rifle and Ted carrying the flashlight. They went for 200 feet or more to where the tunnel made a sharp turn. Following on into it for quite a distance, they finally saw a pair of eyes glaring at them. At that distance and with only a dim light they used up the only four shells in the rifle, then had to come out for more ammunition. On re-entering, they started another barrage and after the first shot he seemed to be coming towards them so Harry fired another quick shot to try to turn him back. When the dust settled they could see he wasn't hit and knowing they had only two more shells they decided to go closer. The next shot glanced off of the top of his head. He seemed to be stunned, but they mistakenly thought he was dead and were about ready to go on towards him when they saw he was up and coming toward them in a semi-crouching position, growling at every step. Well, they managed to get him with the last shell in the gun.

And now for Sewell Goodwin's account, told nearly forty years after the same event:

It was in June of 1961, and it was real dry. I had been at Sonoita and I had heard that two lions had been seen on the Ciénega Ranch and that they had killed quite a few calves. It was just kind of a rumor, so I went over and talked to Fred Barnett, who was the foreman, and Harry Barnett, who was the ranch's cowboy. They led me down to Ciénega Creek to where they had seen these supposed lions. I took a couple of dogs along and they showed me the remains of a calf kill. I noticed something a little bit different in that there was a track in the middle of the water, right in the pond. I could see that it was the track of a cat, but it was very strange as you can trail a lion up to water and it will usually lead to a place to jump across a narrow spot, but this track was right in the middle of the water like it had been laid in there.

I went back and we talked it over. I started hunting in 1950 and I hunted an awful lot with Ted Ferguson of Central, Arizona. I called Ted on the phone and told him I had been to the Ciénega Ranch and that I had seen these tracks that were different. He came the next day or so, and we went over to the ranch. The next morning, Ted Ferguson, Harry Barnett (the cowboy), and I went down to where the calf kills were. We fooled around with the dogs and trailed the area around the track in different places. The track wasn't that great but we were able to follow it up this old two-track ranch road where it headed north down Ciénega Wash. We would trail it a ways, and then we'd lose it; when we did, we would scatter-out, some would go on horseback, some would stay with the dogs.

Harry would go out in front and look for tracks. If he found them, he would come back and we'd pick up the dogs and put them a little bit further in front of the tracks. We were going in a northerly direction, following Ciénega Wash, when we noticed that this track was a jaguar's, as we could see the round pads and that the toes were different from a lion's. And we could also see that it looked like it was leaving the country. We stayed on this two-track road for quite a ways, maybe four or five miles, and we kept on doing the same thing. The dogs could smell it, but they'd kinda stick on it, and then Harry would have to go in front and find a track and come and get us so that we could move the dogs up further. We trailed the cat all the way to the Benson Highway and could see the traffic on Interstate 10. The tracks got close to the highway, maybe half a mile or so, when we lost them. We then noticed that the cat had turned and went up toward the Whetstone Mountains, and at that point we gave up. We could see that the track was getting pretty old so we kinda got together and decided the best thing to do would be to wait until it rained because this animal was leaving the country. Another thing we noticed from this track was that a jaguar evidently travels a little bit different than a lion. He must have been pacing or something because we noticed that when he traveled on the little road, he would turn the dirt up on the track; a lion walks real flat-footed, but this way of moving out of the country seemed to us to be more of a trot in that he would do something to turn the dirt up. The jaguar also made more tracks than a lion would because of his shorter legs.

Well, I went home and Ted went home and when we left we told Fred and Harry that it was definitely a jaguar track and that if they'd like us to come back that would be fine; if they wanted to get someone else to chase it that would be fine too. So we left it like that.

About a month later, in July, I was home at Sunnyside Ranch in the Huachuca Mountains, when Fred and Harry came over and told me that the thing had come back and killed two more calves. Well, I said we'll be there this evening. I called Ted and we met at the Ciénega Ranch at around seven or eight o'clock that night. The next morning we got up early and met in a field below the house where we split our dogs; both my dogs and Ted's dogs hit a track and they went directly north toward this mine tunnel. Now, while we were at the ranch the evening before, some neighbors of the Barnett's, Ed

Hilton and his wife, had ridden over from their ranch northwest of the Ciénega Ranch and spent the night there also. The next morning Ed Hilton joined us, and we all followed the dogs toward this mine tunnel. As we were leaving, we found a note from the driver of a propane gas truck telling us that he had seen a jaguar heading south toward Sonoita!

Now I don't know if it was the New York Mine or the Total Wreck Mine, but it was one or the other, and it was some five or six miles northwest of the Ciénega Ranch. We got to the mine tunnel where both bunches of dogs had wound up. We noticed there were a lot of deer and javelina carcasses in the vicinity, and that even though they had been killed there, none of them had been buried like a lion would do. We made a circle around the mine tunnel, but invariably any tracks we came across would come back to the tunnel entrance. For some reason, the dogs would not go into the tunnel, but kept bawling around the outside as if the animal had been treed there.

We decided that we had to go into the tunnel. The first passageway led 175 to 200 feet straight toward the north, but before we entered, we built torches out of some sotol. We went all the way to the end of that tunnel, but the smoke was so bad, and it burned our eyes so, that we had to come right back out again. After we got outside, Harry took his horse home to get a flashlight as we were unable to find any tracks leading away from the tunnel. Knowing that the jaguar was probably somewhere inside, we tied up the dogs to keep them from trailing all over the country. Mr. Hilton had a gun, a .30/30. When Harry got back, he had also brought some cotton to protect our ear drums. We then regrouped before entering the mine tunnel.

After entering the tunnel, there is a left fork about 60 feet in, and this other tunnel then runs parallel with the first tunnel. Ted and Harry headed on into the second tunnel; the plan was that Harry was going to shoot it and Ted was going to hold the flashlight. When we heard three shots fired, Mr. Hilton said they would soon be back out because that's all the shells there were in the gun. He didn't know that Ted always carried a Luger. But sure enough, Ted and Harry came out for more ammunition. When they reloaded the .30/30, they went back in, as the jaguar was at the end of the second tunnel. The first shot had hit the cat on the right side of the head and dazed him. When we went back in the jaguar was still alive. Our thinking was that if he were to come out we were to face and hug the wall so that the jaguar might go right on by us. But we really didn't know what to do. As it was, the jaguar stayed in the end of the tunnel and we could hear him growl. This time Harry shot and killed the jaguar dead. So much for the gasman's note and his story about a jaguar headed south!

We pulled the jaguar out and he was in real good shape. He probably weighed about the same as a good lion, probably around 140–145 pounds. We measured him, but I forget how long he was. When they counted all the livestock that he was supposed to have killed, the jaguar was credited with twenty to twenty-five calves, a yearling, and a colt. He'd been there for quite some time because some of the tracks were old and you could see that he'd been there for at least that winter.

I have the jaguar's hide. Harry took the jaguar's skin to a Tucson taxidermist to be tanned and mounted, and when Harry died, his wife said it should go to someone who was in the party. Mr. Hilton had died by then, so I paid for it and ended up with the hide. Ted had jaguars he had gotten in Mexico and didn't want it. I was glad for that. I still remember the names of some of the dogs. I had a dog named Brownie, and another named Jake. Ted had one called Butcher, and another one called Rocky. Those were the good dogs, and we also always had ones we were training. I'd only been hunting for about 11 years at that time but Ted had been hunting for a long time and he's the one that schooled me, and taught me the ropes.

The following, and most recent story, involves the photographing of a live jaguar by Jack Childs and his party in the Baboquivari Mountains in Arizona. It was first published in the fall 2000 *Arizona Hunting Tales*. This account is unique, not only because the jaguar was photographed in the juniper tree where he had taken refuge, but also because he was left there intact. This story is also one of the few jaguar hunting accounts with a strong conservation message, an usual event in jaguar hunting annals. And this experience really did change Childs's life. Jack later traveled to Brazil to study jaguar depredation methods, which, coupled with his lion hunting background, prompted him to publish the book *Tracking the Felids of the Borderlands*. This book not only features a collection of tracings of borderland predator tracks, it presents an illustrated discussion on how to identify the kills of jaguars, lions, bobcats, coyotes, bears, and wolves.

Baboquivari Jaguar

By Jack L. Childs

On August 31, 1996, at 7:00 A.M. something happened to me that changed my life. At 5:00 A.M. Matthew Colvin and I saddled up four mules and turned our hounds loose to make an early morning ride in the Baboqui-vari Mountains southwest of Tucson, Arizona. My wife, Anna, was along on this hunt, as well as a young taxidermist named Gavin Weller.

I have been running big game with hounds since 1964 and up until that day I thought that I had seen everything. At that time of year our daytime temperature commonly exceeds 100°F. This was to be a short hunt, mainly to exercise our hounds and keep their feet from getting soft over the summer. Matt had made a hunt in this same country in June, which is our hottest and driest month. He had treed a very large tom lion that weighed 125 lb field dressed with a skull that scored 14 10/16" You hunters from up north will say that this doesn't sound like such a big lion, but here in the Southwest, this size lion is above average. The unusual thing about this lion was the fact that he was badly bitten and scratched up. It looked like a bigger and meaner lion had whipped him. Matt and I hadn't seen the tracks of another tom lion in this area, but speculated that the fight could have taken place miles away. We looked forward to hunting this other lion when cool weather arrived.

Little did we know what was about to happen.

We rode out that morning in the pre-dawn darkness, hoping to make ten or twelve miles before it got too hot. About two miles out, the hounds struck a cold track. These hounds are English blueticks, and are from a line bred from Dale Lee's last stud dog, an English bluetick named Joe. The two biggest males, Music and Flint, struck the track. The little male, Spark, and the two females, Queen and Button, didn't act real interested in working this track. This was unusual, as the females and Spark will normally work a colder track than the bigger males. The ground was real hard and dry, mak-ing it hard for the hounds to trail and hard for us to find a track. As all five of these hounds are trained hounds, we decided to let them work and see what happened. Eventually we found a few partial tracks and decided we were trailing a large tom lion and that we had the right end of the track. By this time the hounds had moved the track about a mile, and all five hounds were working. Could this be the cat that had whipped the big tom? The canyon we were riding up has a good horseback trail running up the bottom. The upper end of this canyon is extremely rough and steep with lots of big rocks, juniper, and oak brush. This trail turns out of the canyon and climbs to the ridge-top on the left-hand side and continues up the ridge parallel to the canyon. Anna and I stopped at the place where the trail turns out of the canyon, leaving Matt and Gavin to follow the hounds into the rough coun-try. We could hear the hounds well from our vantage point. After about a half-hour, it sounded as if they were possibly working around a kill. They would work off in one direction, make a short circle and end up back in the same pocket. After doing this several times, they worked into some bluffs and jumped the cat. After a short race, they treed. Anna and I started up the canyon bottom on the mules. In just a short distance, traveling became extremely difficult and Anna decided she had gone far enough. She said, "I've seen lions before and I'm going to tie up this mule and sit in the shade until you get back." A few hundred yards up the canyon I came upon Matt and Gavin's mules tied to trees, so I tied up, grabbed my video camera and continued on foot. In just a little while, I met Gavin coming back down the canyon. He said, "Matt sent me back for some more film and to tell you to hurry on up there because those hounds have just treed a jaguar." Well, to say that I was amazed would be an understatement. Dale Lee had told me many stories about the ferocity of the jaguar and I was wondering why it had stayed treed so long. I told Gavin that I was going to hurry on up there with the video camera and asked him if he would go down the canyon and get Anna. I sure didn't want her to miss this. Gavin said he would do that and I took off for the tree. That was the longest short climb of my life. When I finally arrived, I could see the hounds and Matt all looking up into this juniper tree, but did not see the jaguar at first glance, so well did he blend in with the tree and surrounding hillside.

When my eyes finally focused on him, he was a magnificent animal. He was lying on a limb, rear end at the trunk with both hind legs and one front leg hanging down. The other front paw was resting on the limb under his head. Matt and I judged the weight of this cat to be over 150 pounds. Comparing the size of the cat's head to the size of his body, we think it was a male. Due to the fact that the jaguar is short coupled and more muscular than a lion, it is difficult for us to be sure about weight and sex. Besides, that was the only jaguar we had ever seen. It soon became obvious that he had just fed and after the fashion of all large cats, had gorged himself. This accounted for the short jumped race and told me why he had remained treed so long.

Matt and I spent the next thirty or forty minutes video taping the scene, praising the dogs and admiring one of God's most magnificent and secretive creatures. At one point, the jaguar laid his head on his paw, closed his eyes and took a short nap, as if to say, "Alright boys, this is boring me. If you would finish your pictures and leave, I will be on my way." Suddenly, the jaguar's ears perked up and he opened his eyes and looked off down the canyon. In a little while, Anna and Gavin arrived. We spent another twenty minutes or so photographing and admiring the jaguar and decided we had better leave. The temperature was climbing and the hounds were growing hoarse from lack of water. Besides, we had pushed our luck far enough. The last thing we wanted was to have a confrontation with this cat, as Arizona law protects jaguars. We leashed the hounds, said "adios" to Mr. Tigre, and went off down the canyon to the mules. We all felt that God had truly blessed us with this less than one-chance-in-a-lifetime opportunity. Oh, by the way, we think we now know who whipped the big tom lion earlier in the summer.

Jaguars in Borderland Folklore

From time to time, it is rumored that a jaguar has become a man eater, but nowhere in Mexico have I been able to authenticate any such report.

A. Starker Leopold (1959) *Wildife of Mexico*

Accounts of jaguars attacking men and their dogs are numerous, most of them involving hunting incidents and wounded animals. Many of these stories are undoubtedly true, and a number of people have been hurt by jaguars in this manner. But, although we have heard of several dogs having been killed while fighting jaguars, we know of no person who has actually been killed by a jaguar. Reports of unprovoked attacks by jaguars are extremely rare, and most of these take place prior to 1850 so that they are now nearly impossible to verify. We are unaware of even a single American newspaper account describing the occurrence of such an incident, although a few such attacks have been documented in South America. Even more unusual are cases of authentic man-eaters. Theodore Roosevelt reported one such incident in his book *Through the Brazilian Wilderness,* and Hoogesteijn and Mondolfi (1993) present convincing evidence that a very young Yanomami child was killed and eaten by a jaguar in Venezuela. These same authors also report an eight-year-old Yekuana girl suffering the same fate. There are a few other less-authenticated cases, but even if true, these incidents must be very rare. When they are reported, the killings almost always involve native children in remote areas where jaguars are lightly hunted. And, with the possible exception of the case mentioned by Roosevelt, no one has ever documented a jaguar that became an habitual man-eater, as sometimes occurs with African lions and Asian tigers and leopards. Nonetheless, the seeming incongruity of there being more records of mountain lions attacking and killing people than jaguars probably reflects reporting differences in culture and geography rather than the number of actual events.

Closer to home, Ernest Lee told Jack O'Connor that sometime prior to 1964 a *tigre* on the west coast of Mexico had become a man-eater and had killed about a dozen persons before being trailed down and shot. This story has never been authenticated, however, and until verified, must remain in the folklore category along with another oft-repeated story of a man supposedly being killed and partially eaten by a jaguar during the construction of El Novillo Dam on the Río Yaqui in the late 1930s. (Ernest Lee also told A. Starker Leopold that the Lee brothers had encountered a number of grizzlies in the Sierra del Nido in Chihuahua, when in fact none of the Lees had ever taken a grizzly, either in Mexico or anywhere else.)

One recent case bears investigating. A U.S. customs official in Douglas, Arizona, Jose Acuña, told Peter Warren of The Nature Conservancy that his uncle was killed by a jaguar near Huasabas on the Río Bavispe. As Acuña described it, his uncle, whose name was Mendez, had a ranch about four hours by horseback from Huasabas. Sometime about 1992 he was riding to his ranch when a jaguar pulled him from his horse and killed him. Apparently another family member witnessed the event, and Acuña's aunt, the widow of the man killed, still lives in Huasabas.

We have also heard numerous tales in Mexico of jaguars following people, just as mountain lions are reported to do in the United States. *¿Quien sabe?* Jaguars and lions are curious animals, and neither is particularly afraid of people if they do not consider themselves threatened. Whether such cases represent mere curiosity or potential malice we will leave to campfire discussions.

The best known borderland legends, however, revolve around the mysterious *onza* (sometimes spelled *onca*). Centered along the northern fringes of the jaguar's range in the Sierra Madre Occidental in southern Sonora and Sinaloa, *onzas* are widely believed to be the product of the coupling of a male jaguar with a lioness. So pervasive is this myth that two entire books have been written on the subject, one by Robert Marshall (1961) and another by Neil Carmony (1995). Even J. Frank Dobie (1949), the Southwest's greatest folklorist, took a stab at describing an *onza* in his *Tongues of the Monte:* "'It is,' the old man replied, shaking one of this sotol stalks in emphatic gesture, 'the very worst animal in the world. Sometimes—sometimes, I say—it is a cross between a bull tiger and a she lion.

Look closely down on this old one's gray legs and see if there are not tiger spots.'"

Depending on the informant, the *onza*'s distinguishing characteristics are a heavily built chest; powerful forelegs; long, lean hindquarters; a soft, wooly, dark gray or brown coat with lighter colored underparts; bell-shaped tassels on its large ears; and yellow eyes that look like balls of fire in the night. When dressing one, an observant hunter will notice that the animal has no small intestine. Like all true hybrids, the *onza* is sterile and the females have no womb, because such an organ is simply not needed. Some people of Yaqui heritage state that the *onza* also has a jewel in its head that shines so brightly as to guide the animal on its nightly forays. *Onzas* hate dogs, and their peculiar whining call is said to lure dogs away from their *rancho* or out of their village, where they are summarily dispatched. All agree that *onzas* are short-tempered and highly aggressive in addition to being exceptionally swift and agile.

Late in the night, as the campfire wanes, still other versions of the *onza* legend emerge. Young girls and women need to be careful about taking too much liquid before retiring, for should nature call during the night and they leave the house to relieve themselves, they, too, run the risk of being raped by a lurking jaguar. And the offspring of such a union is truly hideous. Not only will such a hybrid, or were-jaguar, possess certain wolflike characters in addition to possessing the *onza*'s other features, such a creature will have access to magical abilities more powerful and more dangerous than can be summoned up by any witch, or *bruja*.

Not all of the legends are so sanguine. A wonderful discussion about jaguars using their tails to capture fish was published by E. W. Gudger in a 1946 article in the *Journal of Mammalogy*. Gudger carefully repeated the statements of several observers, who assured him they had seen jaguars flailing the water with their tails to simulate falling fruit, thereby luring the fruit-eating Tambaquy fish (genus *Myletes*) within reach of their paws. Not surprisingly, nearly all of these descriptions depended upon secondhand observations, and most of them had been relayed to jungle explorers by the local Indians. Separating myth from reality has never been easy for would-be jaguar researchers.

We, too, have heard a wonderful array of stories from backcountry Arizonans as well as people living in the Sonoran *monte*. That the devil sometimes takes the form of a jaguar to extract tithes from the living is well known among some rural Sonorans, and it is even whispered that, in the past, lives (no one would say whose) were sacrificed to appease these debts.

It is also well known that jaguars prefer burro flesh more than any other meat. So much so, in fact, that many burros are marked with a stripe down the shoulders, simulating the bloody wounds inflicted by the devil in jaguar form. But because the burro is of a humble nature and the past bearer of Jesus, God allowed the animal to survive these devilish inflictions and altered the markings to accurately portray the sign of the cross, thus insuring against any further assaults.

One long-held myth held on both sides of the border is the presence of multiple jaguars. Whenever a jaguar is killed or even when one is reportedly seen, sightings of other jaguars in the same area are almost sure to follow. Perhaps people prefer not to believe in lone jaguars and they find it more comforting to imagine two or more animals running together. Or perhaps some people are afraid that others will regard their taking or seeing a jaguar to be somehow selfish. These people, still wanting to share their experience, will create another animal for others to see—if not in the present, perhaps in the immediate future.

Another persistent phenomenon is the sighting of black jaguars. Here, too, one report triggers another, until everyone seems to have at least one black jaguar story to tell. The area around Tucson, Arizona, appears to be especially prone to black jaguar outbreaks—at least an especially virulent case of these sightings occurred there in the late 1970s. Although the original reports came from homeowners, who attributed the loss of their pets to a big black cat, the media was vague as to the particulars. With some help from the Arizona Game and Fish Department, it wasn't long before the search was centering on a black jaguar who kept appearing and reappearing in various parts of the city's suburbs. Soon everyone was seeing black jaguars, sometimes in different parts of the city on the same day. Some of the reports were from academics and biologists. Even after the killer, a black Labrador retriever, was finally hunted down and brought to justice, the calls kept coming. Only after the department announced that there was no black jaguar and never had been did the calls gradually cease.

There is, nonetheless, at least one case of a black jaguar in Arizona. Lynn Cool, a hunt guide and all-around outdoorsman, used to run a trap line out of his hometown of Gila Bend. More than once, especially late at night, he would report seeing a black jaguar while making his rounds. More and more often Lynn had to alter his sets in an effort to catch this mysterious cat. Before long other people in Gila Bend were also seeing a black jaguar and reporting their findings to Cool. "Hey, Lynn, have you caught the black jaguar yet?" became a common refrain around town.

Lynn's answer was always the same: "Not yet, but every step he makes is a step closer to my trap." Imagine our surprise one day when the answer to the question was, "Yep, I got him last night. My wife Annie [the town's only taxidermist] is mounting him up right now." A week later Cool held an open house. And sure enough, on the wall above the fireplace was a new head mount of a large cat that looked to be a male mountain lion, except that it was all black—jet black. One had to get real close before noticing the odor of ink and Shinola.

There are other myths, some of which sound almost reasonable. One of the most common of these is that a jaguar in an area will keep mountain lions away, and thus reduce the number of livestock taken. Other ranchers maintain that the jaguar so hates noise that attaching bells to one's cattle reduces, if not eliminates, the chances of the animal being attacked by one of these predators. Jaguars are also said to be more susceptible to poison than lions, a lion never returning to a kill that had been doctored with strychnine or pesticides.

The Jaguar as a Symbol

Jaguar iconography did not cease with the Spanish Conquest. Indeed, it continued uninterrupted. A graphic example is the mural by Rufino Tamayo of the Feathered Serpent (representing daylight and enlightenment) battling a jaguar (depicting darkness and evil) in the National Museum of Anthropology in Mexico City (Figure 59). A contrasting view in the same city is the famous mural by Diego Rivera showing Spaniards lancing a disemboweled jaguar, symbolizing the native peoples of Mexico. Most earlier representations, however, both in Mexico and in the United States, are of ferocious animals in need of subduing (Figure 60).

If anything, use of the animal as an icon has grown until it can now be seen as a logo for everything from dry-cleaning establishments and transport companies to a National Football League team—despite the fact that Jacksonville never had any jaguars in historic times, much less black ones! The most famous jaguar logo by far, however, adorns the luxury sports cars and sedans, formerly made in Great Britain and now built by Jaguar Cars of North America (Figure 61). Sleek yet serene, the Jaguar hood

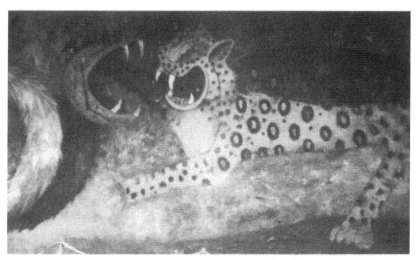

Figure 59. Mural of a jaguar battling with the Feathered Serpent in the National Museum of Anthropology, Mexico City.

Figure 60. Early Colt Firearms poster showing a vaquera dispatching a jaguar.

Figure 61. Jaguar automobile hood ornament.

Figure 62. "Yoco." Courtesy of Luis Gabriel Gonzalez Guedorius.

ornament has long stood for elegance, good taste, and power. Other commercial logos abound, both in the United States and Mexico, where the jaguar is almost as symbolic as the prickly-pear cactus and the eagle. Especially interesting is the recent revival of the jaguar-warrior along the U.S.-Mexico border as an artistic motif both on murals and as graffiti. One can't help but wonder if it isn't time for a friendlier, cartoonlike jaguar to make an appearance (Figure 62).

3

Status and Conservation

The lordly *tigre* will probably persist in the Mexican lowlands
in much better numbers than the big carnivores of the temperate uplands.

Jack O'Connor (1939) *"El Tigre"* in *Game in the Desert*

Livestock have always been the jaguar's bane, not only in the arid
borderlands, but nearly everywhere in North America. This is especially
true in the American Southwest, Sonora, and Chihuahua due to the
scarcity of tropical forests and the fact that almost all of the jaguar's range
is, or has been, grazed by livestock at some time or another. Livestock were
at one time nearly ubiquitous throughout this region and as long as cattle
were present, the jaguar was deemed a predator to be taken at every opportunity. There never has been an area in the American Southwest where
jaguars were protected, including the national parks and Indian reserva-
tions. Although now nominally protected in Mexico, the same general
statement also applies to Sonora, where jaguars are still extant. This incompatibility between livestock raising and protecting jaguars is reflected
in the cat's management history, both in the American Southwest and in
northwestern Mexico.

Management History

Although the territorial legislatures never authorized their coun-
ties to pay for the taking of jaguars, "leopards" were never protected in Arizona or New Mexico Territories. Nor were these animals afforded any protection in the 1912 game codes of the new states. It wasn't until 1919,
when the "leopard" was legally classified in Arizona as both a predator and
a fur-bearer (along with otters and wood rats), that a $2.50 license was

required to trap one. But even this modicum of protection was short lived, and in the new game code of 1929 Arizona's jaguars were again classified as predators and could be killed by anyone throughout the year. This status remained until 1969, when jaguars were designated a protected species by a rule of the Arizona Game and Fish Commission. This protected status has continued until the present time, even though the law was too late to have any real effect—the last female jaguar in Arizona was taken in 1963. Although the Arizona Game and Fish Commission later established a fine for killing a jaguar, it voted on July 19, 1999, to approve the Game and Fish Department's position "not to advocate, support, or permit either a jaguar reintroduction or the designation of critical habitat for the jaguar."

In New Mexico, the jaguar had no status as a state wildlife species prior to 1991, when the State Wildlife Conservation Act included it as a protected animal on its list of restricted wildlife. In 1999 the New Mexico legislature made the jaguar a state endangered species subject to state protection should the animal be downlisted as an endangered species by the U.S. Fish and Wildlife Service. Until such time, however, New Mexico considers the jaguar a federal responsibility. The jurisdiction question is moot, however; a jaguar has not been reportedly killed in New Mexico since 1909.

The legal status of the jaguar in Mexico is more ambiguous. Prior to 1966, the jaguar was considered a game animal throughout the republic with an open season from November 1 through December 31, and a bag limit of one per person. From 1967 through 1972, the season on jaguars was closed except for those holding special depredation or collecting permits. These permits were issued to ranchers and could be transferred to sportsmen, professional predator hunters, or to just about anyone wanting to take "an offending animal." This permit system was subject to much abuse, and no jaguar permits were supposedly authorized in Mexico between 1973 and 1979, when special permits for adult animals were again authorized for the states of Nayarit, Jalisco, Colima, and Campeche, provided that the animals were taken between February 1 and March 31. Although the Mexican government classified the jaguar as an endangered species in 1980, it continued to issue special permits. In 1981, for example, permits were available in the states of Campeche, Jalisco, Nayarit, and Tamaulipas during the period February 1 through April 18. From 1982 through 1985, special permits could be obtained to take adult jaguars in a variety of states, again at various times during the months of February, March, and April. Neither the states of Sonora nor Sinaloa were legally open to hunting after 1980, however, and there has been no legal killing of jaguars anywhere in Mexico since 1987, when international pressures prompted the Division of Wildlife of the Mexican Ministry of Agriculture and Cattle to declare this animal in danger of extinction. Nonetheless, any jaguar deemed guilty of livestock depredation continued to be routinely killed in those states still having these cats. In 1994, in an effort to increase the legal protection of jaguars, the Mexican government included this animal on its official list of endangered species and defined the jaguar as a "priority species for conservation." The only licenses issued are in a special research area in the state of Campeche, where "hunters" pay to assist biologists in treeing, tranquilizing, measuring, radio-equipping, and releasing jaguars. The problem is that there is also a concurrent law that allows landowners to kill any animal, including a jaguar, that menaces their economic possessions, namely crops or livestock. Thus, the jaguar has no real protection from its principal adversary, the stockman.

Not knowing about borderland jaguars, the U.S. Fish and Wildlife Service included only jaguars outside of the United States in their 1972 list of federally endangered species. Accordingly, the jaguar was included as an Appendix 1 species the following year in the Convention on International Trade in Endangered Species, meaning that jaguar pelts or other body parts could not be imported into the United States or any other signatory nation. Later realizing that the jaguar was once also found in the United States, the Fish and Wildlife Service published a legal notice in 1979 blaming its failure to list the jaguar and six other species as an "oversight" that would be rectified as "quickly as possible." Still, it wasn't until the following year that the service published a proposed rule to list the jaguar and four other species as endangered. But then, on September 17, 1982, that proposal was withdrawn, partly on the basis that the service had missed its own deadline to list endangered species under the Endangered Species Act. The service cited higher priorities and its heavy workload for not following up on its earlier promise to list the jaguar. In 1992 a college professor and his students petitioned the service to list the jaguar as endangered throughout its range, including the United States.

In April 1993, the U.S. Fish and Wildlife Service determined that the professor's position was valid and solicited the public for their comments. At that time the Arizona Game and Fish Department concurred with the service, agreeing that the jaguar was at one time a resident species in the state. On the basis of these and other comments and a lawsuit filed by the litigious Southwest Center for Biological Diversity, the Fish and Wildlife Service again proposed extending endangered status to the jaguar throughout its range. It was now 1994, however, and the new Republican-dominated Congress imposed a moratorium on all further listings and eliminated all funding for such activities. Even though the Clinton administration later lifted the moratorium, the U.S. Fish and Wildlife Service continued to stall. It wasn't until the publicity generated by the Glenn and Childs jaguars in 1996 and the specter of more legal action that the service again began moving to list borderland jaguars as an endangered species.

Hoping to blunt the upwelling movement to list the jaguar as endangered, the states of Arizona and New Mexico now requested that the service reopen the comment period on the listing proposal. Both private parties and government personnel feared the legal mischief that might be generated should the jaguar be listed as endangered. Not only might the mountain ranges of southeastern Arizona and southwestern New Mexico be designated as critical habitat, but lion hunting and predator control programs might be banned in these areas. Some even worried that deer and javelina hunting might be curtailed because these activities theoretically could affect the abundance of the jaguar's presumed prey. Mostly, however, they worried that cattle grazing might be more strictly regulated on public lands in the American Southwest.

As an alternative to listing, the states of Arizona and New Mexico proposed to enter a jaguar conservation agreement that would reflect a regional commitment to protecting naturally occurring wild jaguars through the dissemination of information and literature, identifying suitable habitat, and a flexible private-public partnership that would oversee the management of the jaguar. Any of the sixteen or so participating agencies could withdraw from the agreement on sixty days' notice, and the governor of Arizona could also nullify the agreement at any time. Unlike habitat conservation plans, which are contracts between private parties and the federal government and usually allow for some taking of listed species, the conservation agreement was designed to not be enforceable by law. Eager to oblige the states, the U.S. Fish and Wildlife Service reopened the comment period for listing the jaguar, thereby triggering another lawsuit to make the jaguar an endangered species.

An important ingredient of the conservation agreement was the formation of a Jaguar Conservation Team made up of government agency representatives. Assisted by private parties as well as agency personnel, the team was charged with determining the current distribution of jaguars in the United States, formulating laws to increase the legal protection of jaguars, and identifying and protecting existing and potential jaguar habitats. The team was also supposed to promote public education and scientific management of borderland jaguars. Yet, despite the team's formulation of a *Memorandum of Agreement for the Arizona Jaguar*, the U.S. Fish and Wildlife Service listed the jaguar as an endangered species in Arizona and New Mexico (but not Texas) on January 31, 1997.

Both the conservation agreement and federal listing of the jaguar as an endangered species are flawed. Both documents imply that something is being done to manage and conserve jaguars in the United States. This is not only untrue, it cannot be true. At present there is no jaguar population in the American Southwest any more than there is in Texas. With the translocation of jaguars to the United States off the table, the only chance for a jaguar population to naturally become established in Arizona or New Mexico would be for both a female and a male jaguar to travel northward 135 mi or more, arrive at the same time in the same general area, find each other, and set up housekeeping. Such a scenario is so unlikely as to be in the realm of dreams. The fate of borderland jaguars depends entirely upon what happens to the Huasabas-Sahuaripa population in Sonora, Mexico. Should this population disappear, there won't be any more jaguars found in the American Southwest.

Unfortunately, without sound biological information, no understanding of the status of jaguars in Sonora is possible. Although our limited investigations indicate that the mortality of jaguars in east-central Sonora may be increasing, this increase may be a temporary phenomenon due to drought and other special circumstances. Jaguars have certainly shown their ability to persist for a long time in this region under similar conditions. Nonetheless, no jaguars are known to have arrived in the United States for five years, and it is reasonable to think that jaguar numbers in Sonora may be declining. Without any studies into the dynamics of the Huasabas-Sahuaripa jaguar population, its future is strictly a matter of conjecture. However, if numbers have declined, it may well be that the population of females in this area is approaching a critical point. If so, this, the world's northernmost jaguar population, could be danger of extirpation.

Jaguars in Texas and Tamaulipas

Jaguars in northeastern Mexico are in even worse jeopardy. Although the jaguar is listed as an endangered species throughout its historical range, the state of Texas is off limits to jaguar restoration despite the state retaining large areas of game-rich thornscrub (or, as it is locally called, chaparral). Like Arizona and New Mexico, wandering jaguars occasionally visited Texas during the twentieth century because resident populations were still present south in Tamaulipas, Mexico. Now, with the probable extirpation of jaguars in the Soto La Marina and other areas in northern Tamaulipas, there is virtually no chance for such visits. Today jaguars are only nominally protected in Tamaulipas, and those populations remaining in the southern portions of that state may now be threatened. On June 13, 1997, a businessman in Ciudad Mante, who also owned a ranch on the eastern slopes of the Sierra Madre Oriental southwest of Ciudad Victoria, showed us skins and skulls of four jaguars that he had recently killed on his property.

Proposed Jaguar Conservation Plan

We do not believe that the jaguar needs more legal protection, either in the United States or in Sonora, because the present laws are difficult to enforce and successfully adjudicate. Indeed, we do not think that the killing of jaguars must cease. What *is* needed, perhaps desperately, is to reduce the take of female jaguars within at least part of the Huasabas-Sahuaripa area until additional studies can determine the population's status. Once the population's mortality and survival rates are determined, other studies would need to determine the animal's mean home range size and the habitat's carrying capacity. These data could then be used to develop a long-term jaguar monitoring plan. First and foremost, however, is the need to establish a study area so that such research can be conducted. This area would need to encompass the habitat presently occupied by jaguars, be of sufficient size (500 sq mi [1295 sq km] would be a minimum), and provide at least minimal protection for the animals to be studied. Hopefully, too, at least portions of the study area and surrounding countryside would be in a conservation area in which livestock husbandry practices would be limited to steer operations and other livestock management practices more amendable to jaguars than is the case at present. To even partially meet these criteria, the area would need to be located in some of the most rugged country eastern Sonora has to offer (Figure 63).

Designating such a large area as a jaguar reserve would not be easy. Changing the land use would be only one of the problems encountered.

Figure 63. Panorama of Madrean evergreen woodland habitat in east-central Sonora, Mexico.

People are not about to change either husbandry practices or attitudes that have essentially remained unchanged for 300 years. Nor would it be feasible to institute a compensation program to Sonoran ranchers suffering jaguar depredations similar to the one employed by Defenders of Wildlife to aid wolf restoration in America's Rocky Mountains. Any administration of such a program would be nearly impossible owing to the remoteness of the area, the large numbers of depredating mountain lions present, and the difficulty of adjudicating the numerous claims that would result.

Nor will a government-established biosphere reserve, national park, or other jaguar reserve designation be of much assistance. Government reserves in Sonora have been declared with the best of intentions on several occasions, but experience has shown that the administration and maintenance of such sites leaves so much to be desired as to render these actions virtually impotent. Even such basic measures as the fencing and posting of such areas have proven impossible to accomplish. For a reserve of the necessary size to be adequately planned, funded, and staffed requires a governmental commitment that is simply unrealistic given the historical record. To expect the government of either Mexico or Sonora to annually budget and administrate such a site would be sheer fantasy at present.

No, something innovative will have to be devised, something that will involve the local people and not interfere too deeply with their way of life. What is needed is a conservation plan that maintains the present land-use pattern, yet also maintains the take of jaguars at historic levels. Perhaps some *rico* can be found to purchase a core area that can be kept cattle-free for jaguars and native game. Perhaps, too, the *asociaciones*, several of which have proven to be sympathetic to conservation causes, can help persuade a few key ranchers that they will suffer fewer losses if they forgo grazing the rougher *barrancas* and replace cows and calves with steers. At least one rancher has already removed all livestock to rest his rangelands and agreed to allow the translocation of any problem jaguars to his property. There may be others.

One conservation practice that might prove helpful to jaguars would be for a conservation organization to hire a professional lion hunter. This individual would need to be both an accomplished houndsman and trapper and be available to quickly respond to lion depredation reports. Living and working in east-central Sonora, this hunter would pursue and take any lion in the study area that had killed livestock. Should the treed or trapped animal prove to be a jaguar, especially a female, the hunter would either release it or transport the animal to a more suitable area in northern Sonora. This practice, which could be partially funded through the sale of guided hunts, would not only reduce the take of female jaguars, it would also reduce the number of the jaguar's competitors.

There is no antagonism toward jaguars in Sonora, only admiration; yet, jaguars keep being killed. The drought year of 2000 was especially hard on the big cats, when several females paid the price for feeding on livestock. How long *tigres* can withstand such losses is difficult to say. That they have so far is no guarantee for the future. Sooner or later, a limit must be placed on the number of jaguars taken if the animal is not to disappear from both sides of the border. But the truth is that cattle ranching and jaguars are currently incompatible, and the concept of a jaguar preserve is an impractical dream at present. Perhaps someone smarter than us can come up with an idea as to how *el tigre* and his legends can be perpetuated. Unfortunately, it will require a lot more than some Sonoran rancher photographing a bayed jaguar, letting it go, and writing a book about his experience.

Appendix 1. County bounty ledger and affidavit form used in Texas for paying out bounties in 1913.

Pecos_____County, Texas

To____R.C. Marchbanks,_____Dr.

For Scalps of Wolves and other Wild Animals, as follows:

No. Killed	DATE KILLED Mo. Day Year	WHERE KILLED	ANIMALS		AMOUNT
1	Jan 2 1913	Holmes Ranch, Pecos Co.	Lobo Wolves	@$5.00each	5.00
			" "	@$5.00each	
			" "	@$5.00each	
2	Feb 26 1913	Holmes Ranch, Pecos Co.	Grey or Timber Wolves	@$5.00each	10.00
				@$5.00each	
			" "	@$5.00each	
1	Jan 2 1913	"	Panthers	@$5.00each	5.00
			"	@$5.00each	
			"	@$5.00each	
			Mexican Lions	@$5.00each	
			" "	@$5.00each	
			" "	@$5.00each	
			Tigers	@$5.00each	
			"	@$5.00each	
			"	@$5.00each	
			Leopards	@$5.00each	
			"	@$5.00each	
			"	@$5.00each	
4	Feb 7 1913	Holmes Ranch, Pecos Co.	Coyote Wolves	@$1.00each	4.00
			" "	@$1.00each	
			" "	@$1.00each	
			" "	@$1.00each	
			" "	@$1.00each	
5	Feb 12 1913	"	Wild Cats	@$1.00each	5.00
			" "	@$1.00each	
			" "	@$1.00each	
				TOTAL	$29.00

THE STATE OF TEXAS
County of ____Pecos____

BEFORE ME H.L. Winfield, a Notary Public

_____in and for _____Pecos_____
County, Texas, on this day personally appeared R.G. Marchbanks,
_____known to me, who being duly sworn, states on
oath that the foregoing and annexed accounts is true and correct, that it is unpaid,
and that he and no other killed the animals above enumerated_____
(Signed) R.G. Marchbanks

Sworn to and subscribed before me this 27th day of March A.D. 1913.

(Signed) H.L. Winfield

Notary Public, Pecos County, Texas

Approved by the Commissioner's Court the _13_ day of _May_ 191_3_
ATTEST:
(Signed)Frank R. Voney
County Clerk

(Signed)Neswell Johnson
County Judge

ANNUAL REPORT OF GAME KILLED

NATIONAL FORESTS OF SOUTHWESTERN DISTRICT.

1917 - ARIZONA

Forests	DEER		Turkey	Bear	Coyote	Wolf	Lion	Leopard Mexican
	Blacktail	Whitetail						
Apache	14	13	20	8	24	04	15	
Coconino	45	0	49	0	224	19	6	
Coronado	2	115	0	3	119	14	24	1
Crook	0	32	0	2	17	1	17	
Prescott	63	0	17	0	104	0	4	
Sitgreaves	21	0	80	1	53	0	1	
Tonto	32	26	67	9	94	1	13	
Tusayan	5	26	11	1	30	3	7	
T O T A L	182	812	244	24	665	42	87	1
N. M.	295	128	639	68	552	32	40	
District Total-1917	477	340	883	92	1217	74	127	
		817						
District Total-1916	1445		893	62	1364	205	87	

* Exclusive of Peloncello-Animas Division of Coronado.

Appendix 3. Big game killed on Coronado National Forest, Arizona, in 1920.

Supervisor's copy

Tucson, Arizona.

December 4, 1920.

REPORT ON BIG GAME

KILLED ON CORONADO FOREST

1920.

DIST.	BLACK TAIL DEER	WHITE TAIL DEER	TURKEY	BEAR	LION	WOLVES	COYOTES	CATS	JAGUAR
Animas-Peloncillo	2	20	0	0	5	5	20	20	0
Sunset	0	30	0	0	0	0	10	10	0
Paradise	0	95	0	0	4	2	10	25	1
Dragoon-Whetstone	0	10	0	1	2	2	10	10	0
Rincon	0	50	0	0	5	5	25	25	1
Catalina	0	0	0	0	8	0	10	0	0
Santa Rita	0	200	0	1	4	9	75	20	1
Huachuca	0	0	0	1	1	00	10	10	0
Tumacacori	0	8	0	1	3	18	32	24	0
Totals for Forest	2	413	0	4	32	41	202	144	3

NOTE: Ranger Scholefield's estimate of 200 deer killed in the Santa Ritas is considered rather high.

Hugh G. Calkins,

Bibliography

Allen, J. A. 1894. On the mammals of Aransas County, Texas, with descriptions of new forms of *Lepus* and *Oryzomys*. *Bulletin of the American Museum of Natural History* 6:198.

Allen, J. A. 1896. On mammals collected in Bexar County and vicinity, Texas, by Mr. H. P. Attwater, with field notes by the collector. *Bulletin of the American Museum of Natural History* 8:80.

Allen, J. A. 1906. Mammals from the states of Sinaloa and Jalisco, Mexico, collected by J. H. Batty during 1904 and 1905. *Bulletin of the American Museum of Natural History* 22:191–262.

Almeida, A. de. 1990. *Jaguar hunting in the Mato Grosso and Bolivia*. Safari Press, Long Beach, Calif.

Anawalt, P. R. 1981. *Indian clothing before Cortés: Mesoamerican costumes from the codices*. University of Oklahoma Press, Norman.

Aranda, J. M. 1994. Importancia de los pecaries (*Tayassu* spp.) en la alimentacion del jaguar *(Panthera onca)*. *Acta Zoológica de Mexicana* 62:11–22.

Aranda, J. M. 1996. Distribucion y abundancia del jaguar, *Panthera onca* (Carnivora; Felidae) en el estado de Chiapas, Mexico. *Acta Zoológica de Mexicana* 68:45–52.

Aranda, J. M., and V. Sanchez-Cordero. 1996. Prey spectra of jaguar *(Panthera onca)* and puma *(Puma concolor)* in tropical forests of Mexico. *Studies of Neotropical Fauna and Environment* 31:65–67.

Armstrong, D. M. 1972. *Distribution of mammals in Colorado*. University of Kansas Museum of Natural History Monograph no. 3.

Armstrong, D. M., J. Jones, and E. Birney. 1972. Mammals from the Mexican state of Sinaloa. III. Carnivora and Artiodactyla. *Journal of Mammalogy* 53:48–61.

Bailey, V. 1905. Mammals of Texas. *North American Fauna* 25:163.

Bailey, V. 1931. Mammals of New Mexico. *North American Fauna* 53:283–85.

Bailey, V. 1935. Mammals of the Grand Canyon region. *Grand Canyon Natural History Association Bulletin* 1:30.

Baird, S. F. 1859. *Mammals of North America*. Pt. I. *Pacific railroad reports*. Vol. 8, p. 86. Pt. II. *United States and Mexican boundary survey*. Vol. 2, *Zoology of the boundary: mammals*, pp. 6–8. Lippincott, Philadelphia.

Baker, R. H., and J. K. Greer. 1962. Mammals of the Mexican state of Durango. *Michigan State University Publication, Biological Series* 2:25–154.

Barber, C. M. 1902. Notes on little-known New Mexican mammals and species apparently not recorded from the territory. *Biological Society of Washington Proceedings* 15:191–93.

Barnes, W. C. 1988. *Arizona place names.* University of Arizona Press, Tucson.

Barnett, W. F. 1961. A jaguar was caught in Arizona. *Arizona Cattlelog* (August):42–45.

Basso, K. H. 1971. *Western Apache raiding and warfare: from the notes of Greenville Goodwin.* University of Arizona Press, Tucson.

Bennett, W. C., and R. M. Zingg. 1935. *The Tarahumara.* University of Chicago Press, Chicago.

Benson, E. P., ed. 1970. *The cult of the feline.* Dumbarton Oaks Research Library and Collections, Washington, D.C.

Billingsley, M. W. 1971. *Behind the scenes in Hopi Land.* Privately published, housed in Special Collections, Arizona State University, Tempe.

Blair, W. F. 1950. The biotic provinces of Texas. *Texas Journal of Science* 2:93–117.

Blair, W. F. 1952. Mammals of the Tamaulipan biotic province in Texas. *Texas Journal of Science* 4:246.

Boone and Crockett Club. 1981. *Records of North American big game animals.* Boone and Crockett Club, New York.

Boyd, M. 1969. *Tarascan myths and legends.* Texas Christian University Press, Fort Worth.

Brehm, A. E. 1895. *Animals of the world: Brehm's life of animals.* Vol. 1. A. E. Brehm, Leipzig.

Brown, D. E. 1983. On the status of the jaguar in the Southwest. *Southwestern Naturalist* 28:459–60.

Brown, D. E. 1991. Revival for el tigre? *Defenders* 66:27–35.

Brown, D. E., ed. 1994. *Biotic communities: Southwestern United States and Northwestern Mexico.* University of Utah Press, Salt Lake City.

Brown, D. E. 1997. Return of el tigre. *Defenders* 72:13–20.

Brown, D. E., and C. A. López González. 1999. Jaguarundi (*Herpailurus yagouroundi* Geoffroy 1803) not in Arizona or Sonora. *Journal of the Arizona-Nevada Academy of Sciences* 32:155–57.

Brown, D. E., and C. A. López González. 2000a. Search for el tigre. *Defenders* 75:8–13.

Brown, D. E., and C. A. López González. 2000b. Notes on the occurrences of jaguars in Arizona and New Mexico. *Southwestern Naturalist* 45:537–46.

Brown, D. E., and C. H. Lowe. 1994. *Biotic communities of the Southwest: map (scale 1:1,000,000).* University of Utah Press, Salt Lake City.

Brown, J. S. P. 1974. *The forests of the night.* Dial Press, New York.

Burridge, G. 1955. El tigre: plenty cat. *Arizona Wildlife-Sportsman* 26:34–36.

Burt, W. 1938. Faunal relationships and geographic distribution of mammals in Sonora, Mexico. *Miscellaneous Publications of the Museum of Zoology, University of Michigan* 39:1–77.

Burt, W. H. 1961. A fauna from an Indian site near Redington, Arizona. *Journal of Mammalogy* 42:115–16.

Cahalane, V. R. 1939. Mammals of the Chiricahua Mountains, Cochise County, Arizona. *Journal of Mammalogy* 20:418–40.

Carmony, N. B. 1995. *Onza! The hunt for a legendary cat.* High-Lonesome Books, Silver City, N.M.

Carmony, N. B., ed. 1998. *Ben Lilly's tales of bears, lions, and hounds.* High-Lonesome Books, Silver City, N.M.

Carmony, N. B., and D. E. Brown, eds. 1991. *Mexican game trails.* University of Oklahoma Press, Norman.

Carmony, N. B., and D. E. Brown. 1992. *Tough times in rough places*. High-Lonesome Books, Silver City, N.M.

Caso-Aguilar, C. A. 1997. Los jaguares "problema"–-Mito o realidad. *Dumac* 19 (Spring):20–24.

Childs, J. L. 1998. *Tracking the felids of the borderlands*. Printing Corner Press, El Paso, Tex.

Chinchilla, F. A. 1997. La dieta del jaguar *(Panthera onca)*, el puma *(Felis concolor)* y el manigordo *(Felis pardalis)* (Carnivora: Felidae) en el Parque Nacional Corcovado, Costa Rica. *Revista de Biologia Tropical* 45:1223–29.

Coe, M. D. 1970. Olmec jaguars and Olmec kings. Pp. 1–18 *in* E. P. Benson, ed. *The cult of the feline*. Dumbarton Oaks Research Library and Collections, Washington, D.C.

Convention on International Trade in Endangered Species of Wild Fauna and Flora (CITES). 1983. *CITES appendices: mammals*. U.S. Department of the Interior, Washington, D.C.

Coues, E. 1867. The quadrapeds of Arizona. *American Naturalist* 1 (August–December):351–63, 393–400, 531–41.

Covarrubias, M. 1954. *The eagle, the jaguar, and the serpent*. Borzoi Books, New York.

Covarrubias, M. 1966. *Indian art of Mexico and Central America*. Alfred A. Knopf, New York.

Crawshaw, P., and H. Quigley. 1984. *A ecologia do jaguar ou onça pintada no Pantanal*. Relatorio entregue ao Instituto Brasileiro de Desenvolvimento Forestal (BDF)/DN, Brasilia.

Crawshaw, P. G., and H. B. Quigley. 1991. Jaguar spacing, activity, and habitat use in a seasonally flooded environment in Brazil. *Journal of the Zoological Society of London* 223:357–70.

Crumrine, N. R. 1977. *The Mayo Indians of Sonora: a people who refused to die*. Waveland Press, Prospect Heights, Ill.

Cunningham, S. C., L. A. Haynes, C. Gustavson, and D. D. Haywood. 1995. *Evaluation of the interaction between mountain lions and cattle in the Aravaipa-Klonkyde area of southeast Arizona*. Arizona Game and Fish Department, F. A. Proj. W-78-R Rep. no. 17.

Daggett, P. M., and D. R. Henning. 1974. The jaguar in North America. *American Antiquity* 39:465–69.

Dalquest, W. 1953. *Mammals of the Mexican state of San Luis Potosi*. Louisiana State University Studies in Biological Science no. 1.

Dalquest, W. 1969. The mammal fauna of Schulze Cave, Edwards County, Texas. *Bulletin of the Florida State Museum of Biological Sciences* 13:205–76.

Davis, G. P., Jr. 1982. *Man and wildlife in Arizona: the American exploration period*. N. B. Carmony and D. E. Brown, eds. Arizona Game and Fish Department, Phoenix.

Davis, W. B. 1974. *The mammals of Texas*. Texas Parks and Wildlife Department Bulletin no. 41.

Demarais, S., and P. R. Krausman, eds. 1999. *Ecology and management of large mammals in North America*. Prentice Hall, Upper Saddle River, N.J.

Densmore, F. 1929. Papago music. *Smithsonian Institution Bulletin of the Bureau of American Ethnography* 90:54.

DiPeso, C. C. 1953. *The Sobaipuri Indians of the upper San Pedro River Valley, southeastern Arizona*. Amerind Foundation, Dragoon, Ariz.

Dobie, J. F. 1949. *Tongues of the Monte*. Little, Brown, and Co., Boston.

Eisenberg, J. F. 1989. *Mammals of the neotropics.* Vol. 1. *The northern neotropics.* University of Chicago Press, Chicago.

Ely, A. (Chair), H. E. Anthony, and R. R. M. Carpenter. 1939. *North American big game.* Compiled by the Committee on Records of North American Big Game. Charles Scribner's Sons and Boone and Crockett Club, New York.

Emmons, L. H. 1987. Comparative feeding ecology of felids in a neotropical rainforest. *Behavioral Ecology and Sociobiology* 20:271–83.

Emmons, L. H. 1989. Jaguar predation on chelonians. *Journal of Herpetology* 23:311–14.

Emmons, L. H. 1991. Jaguars. Pp. 116–23 *in* J. Seidensticker and S. Lumpkin, eds. *Great cats.* Rodale Press, Emmaus, Pa.

Emmons, L. H., and F. Feer. 1990. *Neotropical rainforest mammals: a field guide.* University of Chicago Press, Chicago.

Emory, W. H. 1857–1859. Report on the United States and Mexican boundary survey, made under the direction of the Secretary of the Interior, . . . A. O. P. Nicholson, Washington, D.C.

Federal Register. 1993. Endangered and threatened wildlife and plants; notice of 90-day finding on petition to list the jaguar as endangered in the United States. *Federal Register* 58:19216–20.

Federal Register. 1994. Endangered and threatened wildlife and plants; proposed endangered status for the jaguar in the United States. *Federal Register* 59:35674–79.

Federal Register. 1997. Final rule to extend endangered status for the jaguar in the United States. *Federal Register* 62:39147–57.

Felger, R. S., and M. B. Moser. 1985. People of the desert and sea: ethnobotany of the Seri Indians. University of Arizona Press, Tucson.

Fewkes, J. W. 1924. *Additional designs on prehistoric Mimbres pottery.* Smithsonian Institution Miscellaneous Collection Publication 2748, Vol. 76, no. 8.

Fewkes, J. W. 1989. *The Mimbres: art and archeology.* Avanyu Publishing, Albuquerque.

Findley, J. S. , A. H. Harris, D. E. Wilson, and C. Jones. 1975. *Mammals of New Mexico.* University of New Mexico Press, Albuquerque.

Freeman, L. R. 1913. Cougar, jaguar and bob-cat hunting in the West. *Overland Monthly* 62:128–30.

Gazin, C. L. 1942. The late Cenozoic vertebrate faunas from the San Pedro Valley, Arizona. *Proceedings of the U.S. National Museum* 92:475–518.

Gentry, H. S. 1963. *The Warihio Indians of Sonora-Chihuahua: an ethnographic survey.* Smithsonian Institution Anthropology Paper no. 65; Bureau of American Ethnology Bulletin no. 186.

Giddings, R. W. 1959. *Yaqui myths and legends.* University of Arizona Press, Tucson.

Gifford, E. W. 1932. The southeastern Yavapai. *University of California Publications in American Archaeology and Ethnology* 29:177–252.

Gifford, E. W. 1936. Northeastern and western Yavapai. *University of California Publications in American Archaeology and Ethnology* 34:247–354.

Girmendonk, A. L. 1994. *Cat sightings in Arizona and Sonora, Mexico: ocelot (1887–1994), jaguar (1848–1994), and jaguarundi (1938–1994).* Nongame and Endangered Wildlife Program, Arizona Game and Fish Department, Phoenix.

Glenn, W. 1996. *Eyes of fire: encounter with a borderlands jaguar.* Printing Corner Press, El Paso, Tex.

Goetze, J. R. 1998. *The mammals of the Edwards Plateau, Texas.* Museum of Texas Tech University Special Publication no. 41.

Goldman, E. A. 1932. The jaguars of North America. *Proceedings of the Biological Society of Washington* 45:143–46.

Goldman, E. A. 1939. Hunting the jaguar. Pp. 421–26 *in* A. Ely et al., eds. *North American big game.* Scribner's and Sons and Boone and Crockett Club, New York.

Gonyea, W. J. 1976. Adaptive differences in the body proportions of large felids. *Acta Anatomica* 96:81–96.

Gonyea, W. J. 1978. Functional implications of felid forelimb anatomy. *Acta Anatomica* 102:111–21.

Gonyea, W. J., and R. Ashworth. 1975. The form and function of retractile claws in the Felidae and other representative carnivorans. *Journal of Morphology* 145:229–38.

Goodwin, G. 1942. *The social organization of the Western Apache.* University of Chicago Press, Chicago.

Goodwin, G. G. 1969. *Mammals from the state of Oaxaca, Mexico, in the American Museum of Natural History.* Bulletin of the American Museum of Natural History no. 141.

Granger, B. H. 1983. *Arizona's names: "x" marks the place.* Treasure Chest, Tucson.

Grinnell, J. B. 1933. Mammals of California. *University of California Publications in Zoology* 40:114.

Grittinger, T. F., and D. L. Schultz. 1994. Social behavior of adult jaguars (*Panthera onca* L.) at the Milwaukee County Zoo. *Transactions of the Wisconsin Academy of Sciences, Arts and Letters* 82:73–81.

Gudger, E. W. 1946. Does the jaguar use his tail as a lure in fishing. *Journal of Mammalogy* 27:37–49.

Guggisberg, C. A. W. 1975. *Wild cats of the world.* Taplinger, New York.

Guilday, J. E., and H. McGinnis. 1972. Jaguar *(Panthera onca)* from Big Bone Cave, Tennessee and east-central North America. *Bulletin of the National Speleology Society* 34:1–14.

Hall, E. R. 1981. *The mammals of North America.* Vol. 2. 2d ed. John Wiley and Sons, New York.

Halloran, A. F. 1946. The carnivores of the San Andres Mountains, New Mexico. *Journal of Mammalogy* 27:154–61.

Heald, W. 1955. El tigre—killer. *Arizona Wildlife-Sportsman* (August):22–25.

Helfritz, H. 1968. *Mexican cities of the gods.* Praeger, New York.

Hewett, E. L. 1938. *Pajarito Plateau and its ancient people.* University of New Mexico Press, Albuquerque.

Hibben, F. C. 1975. *Kiva art of the Anasazi at Pottery Mound.* KC Publications, Las Vegas, Nev.

Hill, J. 1942. Notes on mammals of northeastern New Mexico. *Journal of Mammalogy* 23:78.

Hilton, J. W. 1947. *Sonora sketch book.* Macmillan, New York.

Hittell, T. H. 1860. *The adventures of James Capen Adams, mountaineer and grizzly bear hunter of California.* Towne and Bacon, San Francisco.

Hock, R. J. 1955. Southwestern exotic felids. *American Midland Naturalist* 53:324–28.

Hodge, F. W. 1910. *Handbook of American Indians north of Mexico.* Smithsonian Institution Bureau of American Ethnology Bulletin no. 30, Pts. 1 and 2.

Hoffmeister, D. F. 1971. *Mammals of Grand Canyon.* University of Illinois Press, Urbana.

Hoffmeister, D. F. 1986. *Mammals of Arizona.* University of Arizona Press, Tucson, and Arizona Game and Fish Department, Phoenix.

Hoffmeister, D. F., and W. W. Goodpaster. 1954. The mammals of the Huachuca Mountains, southeastern Arizona. *Illinois Biological Monograph* 24:1–85.

Holt, E. G. 1932. Swimming cats. *Journal of Mammalogy* 13:72–73.

Hoogesteijn, R., and E. Mondolfi. 1993. *The jaguar.* Armitano Editores, Caracas, Venezuela.

Hoogesteijn, R., and E. Mondolfi. 1996. Body mass and skull measurements in four jaguar populations and their prey base. *Bulletin of the Florida Museum of Natural History* 39:195–219.

Housholder, R. 1958. Arizona jaguars. *Arizona Wildlife-Sportsman* (August):14–18, 55.

Housholder, R. 1975. Arizona jaguars (revised to March 1974). One-page mimeo of jaguars killed in Arizona. Privately published and distributed.

Humboldt, A. von 1853. *A personal narrative of travels to the equinoctal regions of America during 1799–1804.* Vol. 2. H. G. Bohn, London.

Hunt, H. 1967. Growth rate of a new-born, hand-reared jaguar, *Panthera onca,* at Topeka Zoo. *International Zoo Yearbook* 7:147–48.

Iriarte, J. A., W. L. Franklin, W. E. Johnson, and K. H. Redford. 1991. Biogeographic variation of food habits and body size of the American puma *(Felis concolor).* *Oecologia* 85:185–90.

Johnson, J. B. 1950. The Opata: an inland tribe of Sonora. *University of New Mexico Publications in Anthropology* 6:1–50.

Julyan, R. 1998. *The place names of New Mexico.* Rev. ed. University of New Mexico Press, Albuquerque.

Kennerly, C. B. R. 1856. Report on the zoology of the expedition. Pp. 5–17 *in* Vol. 4, Reports of explorations and surveys . . . 33rd Congr., 2d sess., House Ex. Doc. 91.

Kiltie, R. A. 1984. Size ratios among sympatric neotropical cats. *Oecologia* 61:411–16.

Kitchener, A. 1991. *The natural history of cats.* Comstock, Ithaca, N.Y.

Knipe, T. 1890–1912. *Collection of wildlife references in the* Arizona Star. Arizona Historical Society, Tucson.

Kubler, G. 1970. Jaguars in the Valley of Mexico. Pp. 19–49 *in* E. P. Benson, ed. *The cult of the feline.* Dumbarton Oaks Research Library and Collections, Washington, D.C.

Kürten, B. 1965. The Pleistocene Felidae of Florida. *Bulletin of the Florida State Museum* 9:215–73.

Kürten, B. 1973. Pleistocene jaguars in North America. Comment. *Biologicae Society of Science Fennica* 62:1–23.

Kürten, B., and E. Anderson. 1980. *Pleistocene mammals of North America.* Columbia University Press, New York.

Lange, K. I. 1960. The jaguar in Arizona. *Transactions of the Kansas Academy of Sciences* 63:96–101.

Larson, S. E. 1997. Taxonomic re-evaluation of the jaguar. *Zoo Biology* 16:107–20.

Lee, C., and A. LeCount. 1970. Jaguar, *Felis onca.* Pp. 111–15 *in Arizona Wildlife Federation record book.* Arizona Wildlife Federation, Tempe.

Leopold, A. 1949. *A Sand County almanac with sketches here and there.* Oxford University Press, New York.

Leopold, A. S. 1955. Appendix 5: the range of the jaguar in Mexico. *Smithsonian Institution Bureau of American Ethnology Bulletin* 170:20–291.

Leopold, A. S. 1959. *Wildlife of Mexico.* University of California Press, Berkeley.

Lewis, N. L., and M. Cupell, eds. 2000. *Arizona wildlife trophies: millennium edition.* Arizona Wildlife Federation, Tempe.

Lindsay, E. H., and N. T. Tessman. 1974. Cenozoic vertebrate localities and faunas in Arizona. *Journal of Arizona Academy of Sciences* 9:3–24.

Logan, K. A., L. L. Sweanor, T. K. Ruth, and M. G. Hornocker. 1996. *Cougars of the San Andres Mountains, New Mexico.* Project W-28R, New Mexico Department of Game and Fish, Santa Fe.

López González, C. A., and D. E. Brown. 2001. Distribución y estado actual del jaguar *(Panthera onca)* en el noroeste de México. *In* R. A. Medellán, C. Chetkiewicz, A. Rabinowitz, K. H. Redford, J. G. Robinson, E. W. Sanderson, and A. Taber, eds. *El jaguar en el nuevo milenio: una evaluación de su condición actual, historia natural y prioridades para su conservación.* Fondo de Cultura Económica, the Wildlife Conservation Society, and UNAM, México, D.F.

López González, C. A., and A. González-Romero. 1998. A synthesis of current literature and knowledge about the ecology of the puma *(Puma concolor* Linnaeus). *Acta Zoologica de Mexicana* n.s. 75:171–90.

López González, C. A., A. González-Romero, and J. W. Laundré. 1998. Range extension of the bobcat *(Lynx rufus)* in Jalisco, Mexico. *Southwestern Naturalist* 43:103–05.

López González, C. A., D. E. Brown, and G. Lorenzana Piña. 2000. El jaguar en Sonora: desapareciendo o solamente desconocido. *Especies* 9(3):19–23.

López-Soto, J. H., O. C. Rosas-Rosas, and J. A. Niño Ramírez. 1997. El Jaguar *(Panthera onca veraecrucis)* en Nuevo León, México. *Revista Mexicana de Mastozoologia* 2:126–28.

Lowery, G. H., Jr. 1974. *The mammals of Louisiana and its adjacent waters.* Louisiana State University Press, Baton Rouge.

Malkin, B. 1962. *Seri ethnozoology.* Occasional Paper of the Idaho State College Museum no. 7.

Marshall, R. E. 1961. *The onza: the story of the search for the mysterious cat of the Mexican Highlands.* Exposition Press, New York.

Mason, J. A. 1952. The Tepehuán of northern Mexico. Pp. 217–24 *in* B. C. Hedrick, J. C. Kelley, and C. L. Riley, eds. *The North American frontier.* Southern Illinois University Press, Carbondale.

Matson, J. O., and R. H. Baker. 1986. *Mammals of Zacatecas.* Museum of Texas Tech University Special Publication no. 24.

McBride, R. T. 1973. *The status and ecology of the mountain lion* (Felis concolor stanleyana) *of the Texas-Mexico border.* M.S. thesis, Sul Ross State University, Alpine, Tex.

McCrady, E. 1951. New finds of Pleistocene jaguar skeletons from Tennessee caves. *Proceedings of the U.S. National Museum, Washington, D.C.* 101(3287):487–511.

McCurdy, R. L. 1979. *Life of the greatest guide.* Blue River Graphics, Phoenix.

McFarland, E. F. 1974. *Wilderness of the Gila.* University of New Mexico Press, Albuquerque.

McGee, W. J. 1895–1896. *The Seri Indians.* Bureau of American Ethnology Bulletin no. 17.

McMahan, L. R. 1986. The international cat trade. Pp. 461–88 *in* S. D. Miller and D. D. Everett, eds. *Cats of the world.* National Wildlife Federation, Washington, D.C.

McNab, B. K. 1971. On the ecological significance of Bergmann's rule. *Ecology* 52:845–54.

Mearns, E. A. 1901. The American jaguars. *Proceedings of the Biological Society of Washington* 14:137–43.

Mearns, E. A. 1907. *Mammals of the Mexican boundary of the United States.* Bulletin of the U.S. National Museum no. 56.

Melquist, W. E. 1984. *Status survey of otters (Lutrinae) and spotted cats (Felidae) in Latin America.* International Union for the Conservation of Nature Report no. 269.

Merriam, C. H. 1919. Is the jaguar entitled to a place in the California fauna? *Journal of Mammalogy* 1:38–40.

Miller, G. S., Jr., and R. Kellogg. 1955. *List of North American recent mammals.* U.S. National Museum Bulletin no. 205.

Minelli, L. L. 1989. *The Olmec: mother culture of Mesoamerica.* Rizzoli, New York.

Molina-M., F. 1972. *Nombres Indigenas de Sonora y su Traducción al Español.* Colonia La Huerta, Hermosillo, Sonora.

Molina-M., F. 1989. *Diccionario de flora y fauna Ingigena de Sonora.* Gobierno del Estdo de Sonora y el Instituto Sonorense de Cultura, Hermosillo.

Mondolfi, E., and R. Hoogesteijn. 1986. Notes on the biology and status of the jaguar in Venezuela. Pp. 85–123 *in* S. D. Miller and D. D. Everett, eds. *Cats of the world: biology, conservation, and management.* National Wildlife Federation, Washington, D.C.

Musgrave, M. E. 1921. Predatory animals in Arizona. *American Game Protective Association Bulletin* 10:11–12.

Nelson, E. W. 1916. Larger North American mammals. *National Geographic* 30:413–14.

Nelson, E. W., and E. A. Goldman. 1933. Revision of the jaguars. *Journal of Mammalogy* 14:221–40.

Nentvig, J. 1980. *Rudo ensayo: a description of Sonora and Arizona in 1764.* University of Arizona Press, Tucson.

Nichol, A. A. 1936. Large predator animals. *Bulletin of the University of Arizona* 7:70–74.

Nowak, R. M. 1973. A possible occurrence of the jaguar in Louisiana. *Southwestern Naturalist* 17:430–32.

Nowak, R. M. 1975. Retreat of the jaguar. *National Parks Conservation Magazine* 49:10–13.

Nowak, R. M. 1994. Jaguars in the United States. *Endangered Species Technical Bulletin* 19:5–6.

Nowell, K., and P. Jackson, eds. 1996. The Americas. Pp. 114–48 *in Wild cats: status, survey, and conservation plan.* International Union for the Conservation of Nature, Gland, Switzerland.

Nuñez, R., R. B. Miller, and F. Lindzey. 1997. Home range, activity, and habitat use by jaguars and pumas in a neotropical dry forest of Mexico. Paper presented at the 7th International Theriological Congress, September 6–11, Acapulco.

O'Connor, J. 1939. *Game in the desert.* Derrydale Press, New York.

O'Connor, J. 1961. *The big game animals of North America.* Outdoor Life Books and E. P. Dutton and Co., New York.

Oesch, R. D. 1969. Fossil Felidae and Machairodontidae from two Missouri caves. *Journal of Mammalogy* 50:367–68.

Oliveira, de T. G. 1993. *Neotropical cats: ecology and conservation.* EDUFMA, São Luís, Brazil.

O'Mara, R. 1997. Jaguar. *Virginia Quarterly Review* 73:307–13.

Opler, M. E. 1965. *An Apache life-way: the economic, social, and religious institutions of the Chiricahua Indians.* Cooper Square, New York.

Ortega-Huerta, M. A., and K. E. Medley. 1999. Landscape analysis of jaguar *(Panthera onca)* habitat using sighting records in the Sierra de Tamaulipas, Mexico. *Environmental Conservation* 26:257–69.

Paradiso, J. L. 1972. Status report on cats (Felidae) of the world, 1971. *U.S. Bureau of Sport Fisheries and Wildlife Special Scientific Report on Wildlife* 4:1–43.

Pattie, J. O. 1905. Pattie's personal narrative of a voyage to the Pacific and in Mexico, June 20, 1824–Aug. 30, 1830. Pp. 1–324 *in Early western travels, 1748–1846.* Vol. 18. Arthur H. Clark, Cleveland, Ohio.

Pearce, T. M., ed. 1965. *New Mexico place names: a geographical dictionary.* University of New Mexico Press, Albuquerque.

Peetz, A., M. A. Norconk, and W. G. Kinzey. 1992. Predation by jaguar on howler monkeys *(Alouatta seniculus)* in Venezuela. *American Journal of Primatology* 28:223–28.

Pennington, C. W. 1969. *The Tepehuán of Chihuahua: their material culture.* University of Utah Press, Salt Lake City.

Pennington, C. W. 1980. *The Pima Bajo.* Vol. 1. *The material culture.* University of Utah Press, Salt Lake City.

Pfefferkorn, I. 1989. *Sonora: a description of the province.* 1795. Reprint, University of Arizona Press, Tucson.

Phillips, J. M. 1913. Transplanting the jungle king. *In the Open* 4(4):13–29.

Piña Chán, R. 1989. *A guide to Mexican archeology.* Editorial Minutiae Mexicana, México, D.F.

Pocock, R. I. 1939. The races of jaguar *(Panthera onca) Novitiates Zoologicae* 41: 406–22.

Quigley, H. B., and P. G. Crawshaw Jr. 1992. A conservation plan for jaguar *(Panthera onca)* in the pantanal region in Brazil. *Biological Conservation* 61:149–57.

Rabinowitz, A. 1986a. Jaguar predation on domestic livestock in Belize. *Wildlife Society Bulletin* 14:170–74.

Rabinowitz, A. 1986b. *Jaguar: struggle and triumph in the jungles of Belize.* Arbor House, New York.

Rabinowitz, A. 1999. The present status of jaguars *(Panthera onca)* in the southwestern United States. *Southwestern Naturalist* 44:96–100.

Rabinowitz, A., and B. Nottingham. 1986. Ecology and behavior of the jaguar *(Panthera onca)* in Belize, Central America. *Journal of Zoology, London (A)* 210:149–59.

Rea, A. M. 1998. *Folk mammalogy of the northern Pimans.* University of Arizona Press, Tucson.

Reichel-Dolmatoff, G. 1970. The feline motif in prehistoric San Agustín sculpture. Pp. 51–62 *in* E. P. Benson, ed. *The cult of the feline.* Dumbarton Oaks Research Library and Collections, Washington, D.C.

Reneau, J., and S. C. Reneau, eds. 1993. *Records of North American big game.* 10th ed. Boone and Crockett Club, Missoula, Mont.

Roosevelt, K. 1939. Hunting the jaguar. Pp. 426–31 *in* A. Ely et al., eds. *North American big game.* Scribner's and Sons and Boone and Crockett Club, New York.

Roosevelt, T. R. 1914. *Through the Brazilian wilderness.* Scribners, New York.

Sadleir, R. M. F. S. 1966. Notes on reproduction in the larger Felidae. *International Zoo Yearbook* 6:184–87.

Safari Club International. 1997. *The SCI record book of trophy animals.* Vol. 2. *All continents except Africa.* 9th ed. Safari Club International, Tucson.

Sage, R. B. 1857. *Rocky Mountain life.* Donohue, Henneberry, and Co., Chicago.

Saunders, N. J. 1994. Predators of culture: jaguar symbolism and Mesoamerican elites. *World Archeology* 26:104–17.

Saxton, D., L. Saxton, and S. Enos. 1983. *Dictionary: Papago/Pima–English; O'ottham-Mil-gahn; English–Papago/Pima; Mil-gahn-O'ottham.* University of Arizona Press, Tucson.

Schaller, G. B., and P. G. Crawshaw. 1980. Movement patterns of jaguars. *Biotropica* 12:161–68.

Schufeldt, R. W. 1921. The mountain lion, ocelots, lynxes, and their kin. *American Forestry* 27:629–36.

Schultz, C. B., L. D. Martin, and M. R. Schultz. 1985. A Pleistocene jaguar from north-central Nebraska. *Transactions of the Nebraska Academy of Sciences* 13:93–98.

Schmidley, D. J. 1977. *The mammals of Trans-Pecos Texas.* Texas A&M University Press, College Station.

Schmidley, D. J. 1983. *Texas mammals east of the Balcones Fault Zone.* Texas A&M University Press, College Station.

Seager, S. W., and C. N. Demorest. 1978. Reproduction of captive wild carnivores. Pp. 667–776 *in* M. Fowler, ed. *Zoo and wild animal medicine.* W. B. Saunders, Philadelphia.

Seaman, P. D. 1982. Hopi dictionary. Draft. Arizona Historical Foundation, Arizona State University, Tempe.

Seton, E. T. 1920. The jaguar in Colorado. *Journal of Mammalogy* 1:241.

Seton, E. T. 1929. *Lives of game animals.* Vol. 1, Pt. 1. *Cats, wolves, and foxes.* Doubleday, Doran and Co., Garden City, N.J.

Seymour, K. L. 1989. *Panthera onca.* Mammalian Species no. 340.

Seymour, K. L. 1999. Size change in North American Quaternary jaguars. Pp. 343–72 *in* R. A. Martin and A. D. Barnosky, eds. *Morphological change in Quaternary mammals of North America.* University of Cambridge Press, Cambridge, U.K.

Shaw, C. A. 1981. *The Middle Pleistocene El Golfo local fauna from northwestern Sonora, Mexico.* M.S. thesis, California State University, Long Beach.

Shaw, H. G. 1983. Mountain lion field guide. *Arizona Game and Fish Department Special Report* 9:1–37.

Sheldon, C. H. 1993. *The wilderness of the Southwest: Charles Sheldon's quest for desert bighorn sheep and adventures with the Havasupai and Seri Indians.* University of Utah Press, Salt Lake City.

Simplich, G. 1919. A Mexican land of Canaan: marvelous riches of the wonderful west coast of our neighbor republic. *National Geographic* 36:319.

Simpson, G. G. 1941a. Discovery of jaguar bones and footprints in a cave in Tennessee. *American Museum Novitiates* 1131:1–12.

Simpson, G. G. 1941b. Large Pleistocene felines of North America. *American Museum Novitiates* 1136:1–27.

Simpson, G. G. 1945. *The principles of classification and a classification of mammals.* American Museum of Natural History Bulletin no. 85.

Smith, W. 1952. *Kiva mural decorations at Awatovi and Kawaika-a, with a survey of other wall paintings in the Pueblo Southwest.* Harvard University, Peabody Museum of American Archeology and Ethnology Papers Vol. 37.

Sonnichsen, C. L. 1974. *Colonel Greene and the Copper Skyrocket.* University of Arizona Press, Tucson.

Spicer, E. H. 1985. *The Yaquis: a cultural history.* University of Arizona Press, Tucson.

Spier, L. 1970. *Yuman tribes of the Gila River.* Cooper Square, New York.

Strong, W. D. 1926. Indian records of California carnivores. *Journal of Mammalogy* 7:59.

Swank, W. G., and J. G. Teer. 1989. Status of the jaguar. *Oryx* 23:14–21.

Taber, A. B., A. J. Novaro, N. Neris, and F. H. Colman. 1997. The food habits of sympatric jaguar and puma in the Paraguayan Chaco. *Biotropica* 29:204–13.

Taube, K. 1993. *Aztec and Maya myths.* British Museum Press, London, and University of Texas Press, Austin.

Taylor, W. P. 1947. Recent record of the jaguar in Texas. *Journal of Mammalogy* 28:66.

Taylor, W. P., and W. B. Davis. 1947. The mammals of Texas. *Texas Game, Fish and Oyster Commission Bulletin* 27:35.

Tellez-Giron, G., and W. López-Forment. 1995. *Panthera onca veraecrucis* (Carnivora: Felidae) en Queretaro, Mexico. *Revista Mexicana de Mastozoologia* 1:73–75.

Treutlein, T. E. 1949. *Ignaz Pfefferkorn's Sonora: a description of the province.* University of New Mexico Press, Albuquerque.

Turner, A. 1997. *The big cats and their fossil relatives: an illustrated guide to their evolution and natural history.* Columbia University Press, New York.

Uplegger, F. J. 1990. *Apache dictionary.* 4 vols. Mimeo. Arizona Historical Foundation, Arizona State University, Tempe.

Van Rossem, A. J. 1945. *A distributional survey of the birds of Sonora, Mexico.* Occasional Papers of the Museum of Zoology, Louisiana State University no. 21.

Walker, E. P. 1975. *Mammals of the world.* Vol. 2. 3rd ed. John Hopkins University Press, Baltimore, Md.

Warren, E. R. 1942. *The mammals of Colorado.* 2d rev. ed. University of Oklahoma Press, Norman.

West, R. C., ed. 1964. *Natural environment and early cultures.* Vol. 1 of *Handbook of Middle American Indians.* R. Wauchope, ed. University of Texas Press, Austin.

Whipple, A. W. 1856. Report of the Whipple survey of the Southwest from the Mississippi to the Pacific Coast. Vols. 3 and 4, 33rd Cong., 2d sess., Senate Doc. 78.

White, L. A. 1943. "Rohona" in Pueblo Culture. *Papers of the Michigan Academy of Sciences* 29:439–43.

Wood, W. R. 1961. The Pomme de Terre Reservoir in western Missouri prehistory. *Missouri Archeologist* 23:1–182.

Wyllys, R. K. 1931. Padre Luis Velarde's Reclación of Pimería Alta, 1716. *New Mexico Historical Review* 6 (April):111–57.

Xantus, J. 1976. *Travels in southern California.* 1859. Reprint, Wayne State University Press, Detroit.

Acknowledgments

Important portions of this study were funded by the Turner Foundation, Inc., through grant 98-305. Also providing funding were the Arizona Game and Fish Department, the Denver Zoological Foundation, Earthwatch Institute, Idea Wild, the Phoenix Zoo, the Lincoln Park Zoo Neotropic Fund, Lyn Chase Wildlife Foundation, Malpai Borderlands Group, Oregon Zoo Foundation, Wildlife Conservation Society, and private individuals. Portions of the text and some of the data were previously published in *Defenders* magazine (Brown and López González 2000a), *Especies* magazine (López González et al. 2000), the *Southwestern Naturalist* (Brown and López González 2000b), and the book *El jaguar en el nuevo milenio* (López González and Brown 2001).

We are extremely grateful to Jack Childs, Warner Glenn, Sewell Goodwin, and Robert L. McCurdy for their permission to reprint the stories that they participated in, hold the rights to, and/or authored. Without their helpful cooperation, this book would have lost much of its authenticity. We are also grateful to the Biology Department at Arizona State University for providing many of the services and logistics necessary for producing this book.

This book could not have been written without the cooperation of a great many people. Especially helpful in this regard were M. and C. Sergio Alvarez Cardenas, Centro de Investigaciones Biologicas del Noroeste, La Paz, Baja California Sur; Josiah and Valer Austin, El Coronado Ranch, Arizona; Randy Babb, Arizona Game and Fish Department, Mesa; Mrs. Henrietta Barassi, Tucson; Ollie Barney, Green Valley, Arizona; Roy Campos, Cuchillo, New Mexico; Neil B. Carmony, Tucson; Leonel Caro and family, Ciudad Cuahtemoc, Chihuahua; Dra. Reyna Castillo, Departamento de Investigaciones Científicas y Tecnologicas de la Universidad de Sonora, Hermosillo; Cheryl-Lesley Chetkiewicz, Alberta, Canada; Rose Coleman, Blue, Arizona; Kevin Concagh, Tucson; E. C. Conway, Tonto Basin, Arizona; Jonathan "Punt" Cooney, White River, White River Apache Indian

Reservation; Charyn Davis, Tucson; Russell and Ronnie Davis, University of Arizona, Tucson; Evelyn Delgado, San Jose, California; Javier Díaz, Culiacan, Sinaloa; Mike Elliot, Bandelier National Monument, New Mexico; Ing. Edgardo Ezrre, Sahuaripa, Sonora; Robert Farley, Nogales, Arizona; Alan Ferg, Arizona State Museum, University of Arizona, Tucson; Mario Fimbres Moreno, Granados, Sonora; Leslie R. Fragosa-Argote, Tucson; Dr. Juan Pablo Gallo, Centro de Investigacion en Alimentacion y Desarrollo, A. C., Guaymas, Sonora; Warner and Wendy Glenn, Malpai Border Group, Douglas, Arizona; José Antonio González, Ciudad Mante, Tamaulipas; Ing. Juan González Loiza, Hermosillo; Dr. Alberto González Romero, Instituto de Ecologia, Xalapa, Veracruz; Sewell and Lois Goodwin, Glenwood, New Mexico; Jeff Grathwohl, University of Utah Press, Salt Lake City; Christine Haas, The Nature Conservancy, Sierra Vista, Arizona; Lloyd "Red" Harris, Tucson; Bader Hassan, Orangewalk Town, Belize; Chuck Hayes, New Mexico Game and Fish Department, Santa Fe; Jim Heffelfinger, Arizona Game and Fish Department, Tucson; Sra. Eli Hernández, El Chino, Sonora; Efrain Herrera "Loco de los Perros," Sahuaripa; Ramon and Arnoldo Herrera, Huasabas, Sonora; Dr. Frank Hibben, University of New Mexico, Albuquerque; Mircea G. Hidalgo Mihart, Instituto de Ecologia, Xalapa; Thomas Hulen, Desert Botanical Gardens, Tempe, Arizona; Alejandro Hurtado (father and son), Sahuaripa; Octavio Jaimes and family, Divisideros, Sonora; Dr. Paul R. Krausman, University of Arizona, Tucson; Karen LeCount, Klondyke, Arizona; Nancy L. Lewis, Phoenix; Sherwin Lipsitz, Tucson; Dr. Rurik List, Toluca, Mexico; John Littlejohn, Presidio, Texas; Dr. Ken Logan, Moscow, Idaho; Sarah Long, Sussex, United Kingdom; Eduardo López Saavedra, Instituto del Medio Ambiente y el Desarrollo Sustentable del Estado de Sonora, Hermosillo; Gustavo Lorenzana Piña, Centro de Estudios Superiores del Estado de Sonora, Hermosillo; Lic. Benjamin Lostanau, Hermosillo; Laurence "Mickey" McGee, Tucson; Brad McRae, Northern Arizona University, Flagstaff; Mrs. Clara Lynn Merino, Mesa, Arizona; Brian Miller, Denver Zoological Foundation, Denver; Oscar Moctezuma, Naturalia A.C., Mexico, D.F.; Dr. Francisco "Pancho" Molina, Universidad Nacional Autonoma de México, Hermosillo; Guadalupe Morales, The Nature Conservancy, Hermosillo; Ron Mouet, Prescott, Arizona; John Myrmo, Tucson; Oscar Navarro, Rayón, Sonora; Kelly Neal, Arizona Game and Fish Department, Mesa; Roscoe Nichols Jr., Ciudad Mante; Concepción Niebla de Acosta, Alamos, Sonora; Web Parton, Tucson; Terry Penrod, Lakeside, Arizona; Yars Petryszyn, University of Arizona, Tucson; Robin Pinto, University of Arizona, Tucson; Curtis

Prock, Young, Arizona; Nannete Ragin, Denver Zoo, Denver; Dr. Rich Reading, Denver Zoological Foundation, Denver; Patricia Rios, Chandler, Arizona; Eduardo Rojas, Quiriego, Sonora; Caren Rosenblatt, New York; Maria Rutzmoser, Museum of Comparative Zoology, Cambridge, Massachusetts; Gary Sanders, Tucson; Harley Shaw, Chino Valley, Arizona; Gordon Sloan, Willcox, Arizona; Steve Smith, Payson, Arizona; Barry Spicer, Arizona Game and Fish Department, Phoenix; Greg Stover, U.S. Fish and Wildlife Service, Albuquerque; Bonnie Swarbrick, Buenos Aires National Wildlife Refuge, Sasabe, Arizona; Frank Tapia, Guadalupe, Arizona; Ron Thompson, Arizona Game and Fish Department, Pinetop; Ted Troller, Portal, Arizona; Ray Turner, Tucson; Sra. Eri Valdez, Hermosillo; Francisco Valencia and family, Sahuaripa; Lic. Gilberto Valenzuela Duarte, Hermosillo; Jimmy Vincent, Tucson; Thomas Waddell, Armendaris Ranch, Truth or Consequences, New Mexico; the late Jerry Wager, Nogales, Arizona; Peter Warren, The Nature Conservancy, Tucson; Joe Wessels, Arizona State University, Tempe; Lavern West, Forestdale, Arizona; Richard White, Safari Club International Wildlife Museum, Tucson; Rick Williams, Driggs, Idaho; Steve Williams, Arizona State Land Department, Phoenix; Jeff Williamson, Phoenix Zoo, Phoenix; Rick Wilson, Tucson; and Ernesto Woodell, Guaymas.

Index

Adams, "Grizzly," 42
African leopard. *See* leopard
African lion, 30, 32, 128
Agua Brava, Nayarit, Mexico, 103, 111
American Museum of Natural History,
    Tables 2, 9
Arivaca, AZ, 16, 96
Arizona, 5, 6, 24, 29, 31, 33, 36-38, 46, 49,
    57, 58, 62-64, 86-89, 96-98, 108, 128,
    140-42, Tables 1,7, 9
Arizona Daily Star, 34, 86, Table 1
Arizona Game and Fish Department, 22,
    64, 97, 98, 99, 131, 138-39
Arizona Historical Society, 38, 81, 88, 102
Arizona State Museum, 91
Arizona Wildlife Federation, 23, 24
armadillo, 19, 42, 50
Atascosa Mts., 91, 93, Table 1

Baboquivari Mountains, 2, 3, 15, 88, 109,
    125-28, Table 1
Badesi, Sonora, Table 2
Bailey, Vernon, 6, 37, 39, 40, 88-90,
    Tables 1, 8
Baird, Spencer F., 37
Baja California, Mexico, 40, 42, 86
Bandelier National Monument, NM,
    79-80
Batopilas, Chihuahua, Table 3
Batty, J. H.,56
Belize (British Honduras), 17, 18, 25, 33,
    44, 50, 60, 97
Big Lake, AZ, 96, Table 4
Bloody Basin, AZ, Table 1
bobcat (wildcat) (gato pochi), 15, 55, 63,
    64, 84, 93, 100, 101, 113, 125
Boone and Crockett Club, 23, 95, Table 6

bounties, 87, 89, 93, 96, 97, 137
Bozarth Mesa, AZ, Table 1
British Honduras. *See* Belize
Brown, Herbert, 87

California, 32, 33, 36, 37, 40, 41, 42
Campeche, Mexico, 33, 44, 68, 100, 138
Carrizal Quemado, Sonora, Table 2
Casas Grandes, Chihuahua, Table 2
Catalina Mts., AZ, Table 1
Central America, 5, 21, 24, 29, 33, 43, 61,
    69, 77
Cerro Colorado, AZ, Table 1
Cerro La Campana, Sonora, Table 2
Cerro Santa Teresa, Sonora, Table 2
Chamela-Cuixmala Biosphere Reserve,
    Mexico, 21, 44, 45, 50. 60, 61
chaparral, 48, 142, Table 1
Chevlon Canyon, Table 1
Chiapas, Mexico, 17, 33, 44, 71
Chichén-Itzá, Mexico, 72, 74
Chihuahua, Mexico, 5, 6, 36, 37, 39, 45,
    46, 57, 58, 81, 86, 101, 105, 114, 137,
    Tables 2, 3, 7
Childs, Jack, 2, 3, 27, 100, 109, 125-28,
    140, Table 1
Chiricahua Mts., 34, 35, 56, 88, 89-90, 92,
    115, Table 1
Chiricahua National Monument, AZ, 90
Cibecue, AZ, Table 4
Cicom Museum, Villahermosa, 69
Ciénega Ranch, AZ, 92, 119-125
Cleveland Natural History Museum, 114
coatimundi, 15, 50-51
Cody, W. F., Table 1
Colcord, Frank, 94, 95, Table 1
Colima, Mexico, 138

collared peccary. *See* peccary
Colorado, USA, 33, 40, 41
Colorado River, 84, 86
Convention on International Trade in
    Endangered Species, 100, 139
Coronado National Forest, AZ, 96
Coues, Elliot, 86
Coues white-tailed deer, 16, 50-52, 61,
    109, 111. *See also* deer
cougar. *See* mountain lion
Coyote Mts., AZ, 49
Cuauhtemoc, Chihuahua, 39, Table 3
Culbreath, Russell, 48, Table 1
Cypress Mt., AZ, 46

Datil Mts., NM, 33, 41, 89-90
deer, 39, 42, 50, 55, 82, 86, 96, 101, 124,
    140, Table 1. *See also* Coues white-
    tailed deer
Defenders of Wildlife, 143
desert tortoise, 51
Dos Cabezas, Mts., AZ, 22, 100,
    Tables 1, 4
Dragoon Mts., AZ, 62
Durango, Mexico, 105

Ejido La Cebadilla, Sonora, Mexico,
    Table 2
elk, 22, 51, Table 1
Empire Mts., AZ, Table 1
encinal woodland, 39, Table 8
Endangered Species Act, 99, 139-41
Escuinapa, Sinoloa, Table 5

Farley, R.. (Bob), 98, Table 1
Florida, 32
Fort Apache, AZ, Table 4
frogs, 51
Funk, Jack, Table 1

Glenn, Warner, 1, 2, 3, 51, 100, 108, 109,
    140, Table 1
Goldman, E. A., 5, 29, Tables 1, 9
Goodwin, Sewell, 16, 62, 92, 119-22, 124,
    Tables 1, 9
Granados, Sonora, Table 2
Grand Canyon, AZ, 33, 34, 40, 84, 85, 91,
    Table 1

Great Basin conifer woodland, Table 1
Greenback Valley, AZ, 86
Guadalupe Canyon, AZ, 86
Guadalupe y Calvo, Chihuahua, Table 3
Guaymas, Sonora, Mexico, Tables 2, 4
Guerrero, Mexico, 29, 33

Hands, E. J. "John," 90-92
Hands, Frank, Table 1
Harris, Red, 91, 93, Table 1
Harvard Museum, Table 2
Helvetia, AZ, Table 4
Hibben, Frank, Table 2
Hoffmeister, Donald F., 5, Table 1
Hollister, Ned, 89, Table 1
Housholder, Bob, 6, Table 1
Huachuca Mountains, AZ, 123
Huasabas, Sonora, 82, 105, 129, Table 2
Huasabas-Sahuaripa population, 108-10,
    141-42

ID Ranch, WMAIR, Table 1
Indians. *See* Native Americans

Jacksonville Jaguars, 132
jaguars
    aging of, 20, 57, 89, 91
    albino, 17
    black. *See* melanistic
    breeding, 55-56
    calling of, 111-112
    captive, 69, 71, 96
    conservation plans for, 142-144
    cubs (kittens), 15, 34-35, 46, 56-57, 60,
        109, 119, Tables 1, 2
    descriptions of, 15-18
    distribution of, 32-46, 48, 49, 63, 87
    DNA, 28, 29
    feces, 26, 28
    as food (for humans), 82-84
    food habits. See prey
    fossils, 31, 32
    habitats and water, 43-49, 142
    hides. *See* pelts
    home ranges, 26, 29, 57, 58, 60, 61, 142
    hunting, 4, 6, 59, 62, 101-104, 16,
        110-20
    killing methods, 54-55

legal status, 3, 98-100, 104, 138-40, 142
legends, 128-32
as man-eaters, 67-68, 70, 128
measurements of, 15-17, 20-25, 56, 80,
    87, Table 1
melanistic (black), 17, 18, 71, 131-132
pelts, sale of, 71, 72, 74, 81, 83-85, 88,
    101, 114, 139
place names, 35, 87, Table 7
poison, 89-90, 93, 101, 104, 109, 132
poisoning of, 7-10, Tables 1,
prey, 2, 50-55, 61, 82, 89, 111, 130-31,
    140, Tables 1, 2
protection, 137-140, 142
regulations, 3, 97, 137-140
sex ratios, 60
sign, 26
skull, 6, 19-20, 23-24, 29, 64, 98, 106
subspecies, 29
taxonomy, 6, 22, 28-30
teeth, 19-21
tracks, 26-28
and water, 49, 50-53, 61-63, Tables 1, 9
weights of, 20-25, Table 1
Jaguar Cars of North America, 132, 134
Jaguar Conservation Team, 3, 140
jaguar warriors, 74-77, 82-83, 135
jaguarundis, 64
Jaslico, Mexico, 22, 33, 44, 60, 138
javelina. See peccary

Kennerly, C. B. R., 40, 86
King, Lon, Table 1
kittens. See jaguar cubs
Klump, J., Table 1
Knipe, Frederick O., Table 1

La Columbina, Sonora, Table 2
Lange, Kenneth I., 6, Table 1
Lee, Dale (Lee brothers), 20, 98, 101, 102,
    104, 108, 110, 111, 114, 127, 129,
    Tables 2, 9
Leopard
    African, 17, 30, 32, 41, 42, 86, 128
    American, 4, 15, 30, 33, 86, 87, 93, 96,
        101, 137
    Mexican, 86, 93
Leopard Springs, AZ, 87

Leopold, A. Starker, 1, 42, 43, 56, 128-129
Ligon, J. Stokely, 93
Lily, B. (Ben) V., 97, Table 1
lion (león). See mountain lion; African
    lion
livestock, 4, 40, 52-55, 60-61, 64, 82, 88-
    89, 91, 94, 101, 104, 109-111, 120, 122,
    125, 131-32, 137-40, 142, 144,
    Tables 1, 2
Los Angeles County Museum, Table 2

Madrean evergreen woodland, 36, 45, 46,
    63, 143, Tables 1, 2, 3, 9
Marismas Nacionales, Mexico, 44, 45, 56,
    111
McBride, Roy T., 38, 105
McGee, Laurence "Mickey," 59, 96,
    Table 1
Mearns, E. A., 29, Table 9
Mexican Ministry of Agriculture and
    Cattle, 139
Michoacan, Mexico, 33
Miller, Clyde, Table 1
Mogollon Rim, 34
Mogollon, Mts., AZ, Table 1
Mogollon Mts., NM, 89, 115, Table 1
montane conifer forest, 46
Monte Alban, Oaxaca, 69, 70
Moreno Sta., Guaymas, Sonora, Table 2
Morrow, R. Ranger, Table 1
mountain lions (cougar, puma), 1, 4, 15,
    17, 19-20, 26-28, 31, 41, 50-55, 61-64,
    67-68, 70-71, 74, 76-77, 79, 82, 84, 89,
    91-94, 97, 100-101, 103-106, 109, 111-
    13, 115, 119-23, 126-29, 131, 140, 144

Nacori Chico, Sonora, Table 2
National Museum of Anthropology, Mex-
    ico City, 70, 72, 73, 75, 76, 132-33
Native Americans, 41, 42, 67
    Anasazi, 77, 78
    Apache, 82, 84, 91, 92
    Aztec, 73-77, 79
    Cahita (language), 36, 80, 81
    Casa Grande, 77, 78
    Commanche, 41
    Guarijio, 81
    Havasupai, 84

Hohokam, 77
Hopi, 78, 84-85, Table 1
Hualapai, 84
Huasteca, 77
Huichol, 76, 77
Mayan, 69, 71, 72, 74
Mayo, 80, 81
Mimbres, 77, 78
Olmec, 68, 69, 71
Opata , 82
Papago (Tohono O'odham), 15, 42, 83, 88
Pima, 82-84
Pueblo, 84
Seri, 82
Sobaipuris, 82
Tarahumara, 81, Table 3
Tarascan, 77
Tepehuán, 81
Toltecs, 70-74, 78-79
Tupi-Guarani, 4
Yanomami, 128
Yaqui, 15, 80, 108, 130
Yavapai, 84
Yekuana, 128
Yuman, 84
Zapotec, 70
Zuni, 40
Nature Conservancy, The, 129, Table 9
Nayarit, Mexico, 24, 33, 44, 45, 51, 64, 103, 138
Nelson, E. W., 29, 32, Table 1
New Mexico, 5, 31, 33, 35, 36, 37, 40, 41, 46, 58, 86, 87, 89, 96, 137, 140-42
Noon, Walter, 16, Table 1
Novillo Dam, Sonora, Table 2
Nuevo Leon, Mexico, 33

O'Connor, Jack, 20, 21, 96, 129, 137, Table 2
O'Doherty, E. J., Table 1
oak-juniper encinals, 19, 38, Table 8 (see also Madrean evergreen woodland)
Oaxaca. Mexico, 33, 45, 69, 70
ocelot, 15, 27, 62, 63, 64, 99, 113, Table 9
onza (onca), 129-130
opossum, 5

PARC (Predator and Rodent Control). See U.S. Biological Survey; U. S. Fish and Wildlife Service
Patagonia Mts., AZ, 59, 96, Table 1
Pattie, James Ohio, 42, 85
peccary (javelina), 31, 39, 42, 50-52, 55, 82, 109, 124, 140
Peloncillo Mountains, AZ/NM, 1, 86, 108, Table 1
Penrod, Terry, 59, 96, 111, Table 1
Peterson, Ranger G. (Pete), 16, Table 1
petroglyphs, 77, 78
pinon-juniper woodland, 46
Pitiquito, Sonora, Table 2
predator control, 87-94, 97, 101-105, 109, 120, 140, Tables 1, 2
Pleistocene, 31, 32
Prock, C. J., 18
professional hunters, 100-103, 105
Puerto Libertad, Sonora, Table 2
puma. See mountain lion

Queretaro, Mexico, 33
Quierego, Sonora, Tables 2, 4
Quintana Roo, Mexico, 33, 44

Rancho Badesi, Sonora, Table 2
Rancho Cervantes, Sonora, Table 2
Rancho Cuervo, Chihuahua, Table 3
Rancho El Alamo, Sonora, Table 2
Rancho El Carrizal Quemado, Sonora, Table 2
Rancho El Naranjo, Sonora, Table 2
Rancho El Rodeo, Sonora, Table 2
Rancho Guirocoba, Sonora, Table 2
Rancho La Cieneguita, Sonora, Table 2
Rancho La Montosa, Sonora, Table 2
Rancho La Poza, Sonora, Table 2
Rancho La Primavera, Sonora, Table 2
Rancho La Sierrita, Sonora, Table 2
Rancho Las Norias, Sonora, Table 2
Rancho Los Pavos, Sonora, Table 2
Rancho Los Pescador, Sonora, Table 2
Rancho Los Taraices, Sonora, Table 2
Rancho San Vicente, Sonora, Table 2
Rancho Santa Margarita, Sonora, Table 2
Rancho Tabiquito, Sonora, Table 2
Red Mt., AZ, Table 1

Ren, Charlie, Table 2
Rincon Mts., AZ, 87-88, Table 1
Rincon Valley, AZ, 95, Table 1
Río Aros, Sonora, 86, 102, 103, 108, 114, 115, Table 2
Río Bavispe, Sonora, 82, 86, 102, 103, 110, 129
Río Granados, Sonora, 115, 118
Rio Grande, TX, 40, 41, 43, 86
Río Yaqui, Sonora, 103, 108, 110, 114, Table 2
RO Ranch, Sonora, 101, 102
Rocky Mt. conifer forest/Great Basin conifer woodland, Table 1
Rocky Mt. montane conifer forest, Table 1
Rocky Mt. subalpine conifer forest, 96, Table 1
Rohona, 84
Roosevelt, Theodore, 28, 128

Sage, Rufous B., 41
Sahuaripa, Sonora, 104, Tables 2, 4
San Javier, Sonora, Table 2
San Luis Potosi, Mexico, 33
San Pedro de la Cuerva, Sonora, Table 2
Sand Tank Mts., AZ, Table 1
Santa Maria Mts., AZ, Table 1
Santa Rita, Mts., AZ, 86, Table 1
semi-desert grassland, 48-49, Tables 1, 2, 9
Seton, Ernest Thompson, 6, 21, 30, 33, 34, 41-42, Table 1
Shaw, Harley, 19, 22
Sierra Atascosa. See Atascosa Mts.
Sierra Azul, Sonora, Table 2
Sierra Bacatete, Sonora, 108, Tables 2, 4
Sierra Cucurpe, Sonora, Table 2
Sierra de los Caballos, NM, Table1
Sierra de los Chinos, Mexico, 104, Table 2
Sierra del Nido, Chihuahua, Table 3
Sierra El Novillo, Sonora, Table 2
Sierra Estrella, AZ, Table 1
Sierra Frentón, Sonora, 103
Sierra Los Mochis, Sonora, Table 2
Sierra Madre Occidental, Mexico, 45, 81, 86, 110, 129, Tables 2, 4
Sierra Madre Oriental, Mexico, 142
Sierra Picœ, Sonora, Table 2

Sierra Zetasora, Sonora, Table 2
Sinaloa, Mexico, 22, 24, 33, 44, 45, 47, 56, 103, 107, 108, 129, 138
Sinaloan deciduous forest, 47, 48, 63, Tables 2, 9
Sinaloan thornscrub, 46- 49, 63, 109, Tables 2, 9
skunk, 2, 51
Sonora, Mexico, 5, 6, 15, 24, 26, 29, 31, 36-37, 39, 42, 45-48, 56-58, 60-62, 64, 81-82, 86, 95, 97, 101-110, 113-20, 129-30, 134, 137-38, 141-42, 144, Tables 2, 7, 9
Sonoran Desert, 42, 48, Table 1
South America, 17, 18, 21, 28, 30, 32, 33, 43, 60, 61, 67, 87, 125, 128
Southeastern semievergreen forest, Table 8
Southwest Center for Biological Diversity, 139
Soyopa, Sonora, Table 2
Straw, Nat, 89, Table 1
Suaqui, Sonora, Table 2
Sunset Pass, AZ, Table 1

Tabasco, Mexico, 29, 33, 68, 69
Tamaulipan semideciduous forest, Table 8
Tamaulipan thornscrub, 38, 39, Table 8
Tamaulipas, Mexico, 18, 29, 33, 38, 39, 141, 142
Tampico, Veracruz, Table 6
Teotihuacán, Mexico, 69, 70, 71, 77
Tepache, Sonora, Mexico, Table 2
Texas, 5, 24, 30, 31, 33, 37, 38, 39, 44, 86, 93, 97, 105, 141-142, Table 6
Tiburón Island, Mexico, 82
Tombstone Epitaph, Table 9
Tonichi, Sonora, Table 2
Tonto National Forest, 87
Tortolita Mts., AZ, 88, Table 1
trapping, 7, 8, 11, 41, 42, 64, 89, 90, 94, 101, 104, 106, 111, 131, 138, 144, Tables 1, 2
tropical deciduous forest, 43, 44, 45
tropical semideciduous forest, 44
Tubatama, Sonora, Table 2
Tumacacori Mts., AZ, Table 1

U.S. Biological Survey, 33, 34, 89, 93, 95
U.S. Department of Justice, 100
U.S. Fish & Wildlife Service (USFWS), 48, 100, 138-41, Table 1
U.S. Forest Service, 96
U.S. National Museum (USNM), 29, 37, 39, 94, 95, Tables 1, 8, 9
University of Arizona, 98, Table 1

Velarde, Father Luis, 101
Veracruz, Mexico, 33, 68, 69, Table 6
von Humboldt, Alexander, 17
Vorhies, C. T., Table 1

were-jaguar, 130
Whetstone Mountains, AZ, 123

White Mountain Apache Indian Reservation (WMAIR), 35, 48, 91, 96, Table 1
White Mts., AZ, 22, 46, 59, 96, 111, Table 1
wildcat. See bobcat
Winslow, George, Table 1
wolves, 55, 82, 89, 143
Woodell, Dick, Table 2
Woodell, Lee, Table 2

Yecora, Sonora, Mexico, Table 2
Yucatan, Mexico, 29, 33, 44, 72

Xantus, J., 42

About the Authors

DAVID E. BROWN is a wildlife biologist who has worked in the Southwest for forty years and is currently an adjunct professor of biology at Arizona State University. He has written and edited numerous books on Southwestern wildlife and personalities. Among his titles currently in print are *Biotic Communities: Southwestern United States and Northwestern Mexico* (University of Utah Press); *A Classification of North American Biotic Communities* (University of Utah Press); *The Wolf in the Southwest* (University of Arizona Press); *The Grizzly in the Southwest* (University of Oklahoma Press); *Arizona Game Birds* (University of Arizona Press); *Vampiro: The Vampire Bat in Fact and Fantasy* (University of Utah Press); and, with Neil Carmony, *Aldo Leopold's Wilderness* (Stackpole Books); *Gila Monster: Facts and Folklore of America's Aztec Lizard* (University of Utah Press); *Mexican Game Trails* (University of Oklahoma Press); and *Tough Times in Rough Places* (University of Utah Press).

CARLOS A. LÓPEZ GONZÁLEZ is a research associate with the Denver Zoological Foundation. He received his bachelor's, master's, and doctorate degrees in science at Universidad Nacional Autonoma de México. His main interests are in predator-prey interactions, vertebrate community ecology, and behavior and conservation of large mammalian carnivores.